Managing your Workforce

Insights for startups and small business - from a master entrepreneur

New, expanded second edition

Dave Berkus

Published by David Berkus DBA The Berkus Press

For corrections, company/title updates, comments, or any other inquiries, please e-mail DBerkus@berkus.com

Second Printing 2014
10 9 8 7 6 5 4 3 2

ISBN: 978-1-105-04070-2

The content within this book has been previously published within the books, BERKONOMICS, and ADVANCED BERKONOMICS. Individual insights from this book are published periodically in Dave's emails and blog, www.berkonomics.com.

Groups may order copies of the book at a group discount by contacting Dave Berkus at 626-355-5375, or at dberkus@berkus.com .

Throughout this book, the Cambria type font was used for headlines, and text was set using the Calibri font.

Contents

INTRODUCTION

This book is the fourth in a series of eight short, easy to read books that guide an entrepreneur through the stages of creation, management, growth, and ultimately sale of a small business enterprise. And this is the second edition of this book, packed with half again as much materials the first edition, published in 2011.

Each section is an insight into another facet of starting a business that is not taught in business school or available in business texts, but rather the result of over fifty years of entrepreneurial experience with my own entrepreneurial companies and serving as investor, coach, mentor and board member for over forty entrepreneurial startups over the years.

Originally published as portions of three books, BASIC BERKONOMICS, BERKONOMCS, and ADVANCED BERKONOMICS, comments from entrepreneurs and professional managers after reading those books led to suggestions that I create separate mini-books for each stage of the business, to appeal to the interests of those at that stage of development, ready to absorb and implement insights that apply directly to the current stage of their business. Make them inexpensive and available as eBooks, they suggested, so that entire teams of managers could use the book as a planning tool and discussion prompt for the team in meetings.

And so this series of Small Business Success Books was born to address an opportunity. You can pick up this book and immediately relate to the insights, issues, opportunities, and exercises in this book right at the earliest stages of creating your business. This is not a replacement for "how to" books, courses, and consultants. It is a deeper opportunity to evaluate, plan, and execute strategies for growth based upon these insights that augment and amplify the usual "how to" materials available to entrepreneurs.

In this book, I'll tell personal stories from my fifty-plus years of entrepreneurial experience. But every one of us has a story to add to this mix, one of passionate entrepreneurism, sometimes inside an existing larger corporation, sometimes alone on a kitchen table, or back room desk. And it is a sure thing that many of us will have cogent, insightful additions to this caldron, culled from their own experiences. There's a place for these in the blog, www.berkonomics.com, and I welcome any and all for others to read and learn.

Dave Berkus

Arcadia, California

Managing your Workforce

There comes a time when businesses outgrow the original span of control of the entrepreneur. This critical period is a test of the entrepreneur's desire and ability to delegate, after successfully hiring the best of candidates to fill needed slots in the infrastructure. We hire the best people we can find, and turn from visionary entrepreneurs into (sometimes unwilling) managers of people. Most every entrepreneur experiences this as the company grows, even in its infancy.

Allow me to digress to the story of my first hiring decision for my first company, years ago. At that time I was managing a small and growing phonograph record manufacturing business using independent contractors for both content and production. I built this business through my high school and college years. Soon after graduating from college, I was making a good living and enjoying growth and freedom managing the enterprise.

It occurred to me that I had come to a fork in my career. I could continue with the status quo, making a good living, or I could reinvest virtually all of my profit into my first hire, an assistant that would free me from the day-to-day management tasks, allowing me to recruit more business (content) and build a real enterprise. This was a tough decision at that time. Comfort, or risk-it-all? On a Friday evening, I got into my car and drove from my office in the Los Angeles area all the way to Ensenada, Mexico, checking into a remote beach hotel. Early the next morning I found a large rock at the shoreline, climbed it, and sat there for hours contemplating my future. Hire for growth, or grow slowly and comfortably? Well, the decision was what you expected. I did hire my first employee, leveraging her organizational skills to grow quickly enough to continue hiring as growth accelerated. The company reached fifty employees at the point where I sold my interest and moved into the computer programming business at what turned out to be just the right time. But I'll not forget the overwhelming weight of that early decision, compared to the many much more expensive decisions made in subsequent years. I was for the first time dependent upon the work of others. And I had made a successful hiring decision, lucky for me.

As years passed, a number of hiring insights became clear as I made mistakes and had successes, and watched other entrepreneurs struggle with similar choices and opportunities. Let me share some of those insights.

"Over-welcome" your new employees.

A CEO friend of mine who manages her one hundred person remote workforce as a virtual company told me her story of how she welcomes new employees as she grows her firm. *Strike that.* She over-welcomes her new employees.

Days before the official start date, she makes sure that the new employee's business cards arrive in the mail, that the employee's phone and Internet services are up and running, and that an email account is already established. But many of us do that, maybe not so timely.

Then she topped her explanation with: "A few days before the start, a package arrives from us at the employee's home with a welcome letter, a copy of the CEOs book, and a giant fortune cookie, with the fortune cookie message streamer clearly visible."

"You will be successful at our company!" the fortune states.

What a great touch - especially for someone expected to be self-motivated enough to work long hours from home, to get to know fellow employees through Skype and texting, and to be productive immediately when hitting the ground.

It started me thinking. How many days or weeks or even months do we expect a new employee to take in becoming acclimated to our company and its culture, to the marketplace, and to our ways of doing business? For example, most of us expect a salesperson to be truly productive only after about six months of building a territory or client base. But isn't there a better way to approach this expensive process of acclimation?

For a salesperson, how about paying an override commission to another sales person for a short period to help find and close new business? Or how about helping the employee gain confidence by handing the first several accounts to the new person ready to close? How about assigning a big brother or sister to each new employee to show them the culture and process? How about teaching a class in corporate culture yourself to one or more new employees? Some of us have done one or more of these things. But what could we have done better to launch a new employee successfully?

Maybe we should start with a surprise fortune cookie with a personal welcome message.

Don't make assertions that will later prove untrue.

Sometimes it is easy for someone at the top of an organization to make a statement that, in the enthusiasm of the moment or to make a point, crosses the line between fact and fiction. Sometimes it seems to you to be just an unimportant little stretch of the facts. An estimate of the number of customers, of the amount of traffic to your website, of the numbers of products sold or hours spent in development - there are thousands of areas where a number sounds better when it is larger.

Often, the number you state cannot easily be challenged, sometimes justifying the use of a larger number as a way to impress at potential customer, or make a point at an industry meeting.

In this age of readily available information, the risk involved in making a statement that can later be proved untrue is too great. It goes to your credibility itself when discovered or challenged. And often, when someone discovers or uncovers the truth, you'll never hear of it, even as that person lowers his or her trust in your future statements by some level as a result.

Yet, we have all done this in one form or another, some harmlessly, some with intent to deceive. An often-expressed example seems to come from the salesperson who quotes a larger number of users or customers than the facts support. Yes, we've seen gray areas. In one example in an industry I know well, there are direct customers and then central systems that in turn support direct customers. The company in mind provides systems to serve both, but its salespeople count as customers all of the indirect customers served by the one system sold to oversee them. The result is an inflated number of total customers, which when compared to the competition counting only direct customers, makes the company look much larger and with greater market share.

Is there any harm in this activity? Yes, in two ways, this hurts credibility and confidence. Competitors have every incentive to research the truth of your statements and every incentive to broadcast findings of inaccuracies. And the creator of the knowingly inaccurate statement will always be a bit wary about being challenged, sapping just a bit of energy away from other communications with the same constituents, and knowing that a previous statement is vulnerable to attack.

It is best just to not make those statements in the first place. They probably don't do the job expected in enhancing the person's or company's reputation as intended anyway.

Attack critical issues first.

There are two reasons to consider reordering your priorities to attack your most critical issues first, before the easiest ones to knock off the list.

First, you are fresher at the start of a day, and your best efforts should come when you are best prepared to address these issues. Remember how easy it is to put off those final decisions at the end of a tiring and long day?

But the real reason to do this is to allow most everything else to fall into place, once the critical issues are worked out. It's true in every business, all the time.

Take for example, solving key technology problems that prevent a product from shipment, or from scaling to large production. If sudden demand for a product takes management by surprise, having solved these key issues will remove the key barrier to ramping production and taking advantage of the opportunity.

In a young company, the key issue is most often finding the way to start the revenue flowing from services and sales. With enough revenues, the young company can more easily raise equity funds, borrow money, hire top talent, and gain valuable publicity.

Next, a critical key issue is finding the way to break-even for a young business – the proxy for stability. Working on that issue alone can drain a CEO, given its many incarnations - in marketing, sales, finding efficiencies, cutting efforts that are of lesser value, and more.

Hire key talent to develop the product, to create a manufacturing line, establish distribution channels, to organize the sales effort, and you will find that many other less important issues resolve themselves or fall into place, much less important than before the critical issues had been resolved.

Back to basics: **Three qualities of a great leader**

There are lots of ways to measure a great leader. Here are three that should resonate with you as leader and with those who follow you. These qualities are applicable whether you are leading your company or a board, and certainly are aspiration targets for you if you are measuring yourself against the best.

The first quality in a great leader is to have *laser focus*. Every organization has limited resources, especially money and time. So a leader who is able to focus upon the core needs of the organization, eliminating all the surrounding noise, is one who uses the limited resources available to best effect. McDonald's does this by focusing upon good food, delivered quickly. There are a million examples of great companies and their leaders focusing like a laser on core components of the business and succeeding where others failed because of the inefficient use of limited resources.

Second is *consistency*. It is more than difficult to follow a leader who changes course seemingly without reason, or sets standards that change by day or by whim, or rewards one person or department differently than others. Inconsistency breeds fear, disillusionment, and discontent among those suffering, following this flaw in leadership.

Third, a great leader establishes goals that lead all *to maintaining forward progress*. Stagnant companies lose their best employees, those wanting a challenge and upward mobility in a growth environment. Forward progress can be felt by all and celebrated as the company reaches new milestones toward its goals.

Measure yourself against these three qualities. Have the courage to ask a board member or even a direct report to comment on your three measures. Where do you need a bit of work? Not one of these requires formal education. So there is no excuse for failure to be your best in all three qualities.

The five tactical skills of a great executive

While we are on the subject of great leadership, let's list the five principal tactical skills of a great leader. These are not the strategic visionary skills, like leading companies through risky product launches, or steering the course through economic storms where leaders become oversized personalities for their superhuman efforts. These are the skills of daily operation, the ones that make or break a company - from the top.

Think of those leaders from your past or present whom you respect most. Compare their leadership style with these five skills.

Skill number one: *delegate*. Nothing is more of a turn off to a subordinate than having the boss do the work for that person. Worse yet, failures to delegate make the leader the principal bottleneck in the flow of work through an organization. A great leader learns to delegate, first.

Second: *measure the results* of delegation. If there is no attempt to measure, no-one will know if the work is up to standards for timeliness, quality, or the vision of the leader. There are many types of metrics, some very easy to manage. But failure to find and use them regularly is a failure at the top.

Third: *support*. A leader's duty is to make sure that anything s/he delegates and measures is given a chance of success by providing the tools required to perform the job. Those include funding, people, training and facilities.

Fourth: *reward*. A great leader is a great cheerleader, knowing when and how to reward effective achievement through all levels of the organization. People naturally work for rewards, from simple recognition to financial incentives.

Fifth: *celebrate*. There is no greater feeling than to achieve a goal and to celebrate that with some form of out-of-the-ordinary event. It can be a simple handshake and comment in front of others who count, or an all-company celebration after achievement of a major goal. A leader who fails to follow through and celebrate misses a major opportunity to enhance the culture of the organization and motivate the troops to further achievements.

Delegate, measure, support, reward and *celebrate*.

If it can be counted, the CFO owns it.

There is a simple way to define the responsibilities of the chief financial officer. And it extends beyond the usual interpretation of the CFO position in many companies. *If it can be counted, the CFO owns the responsibility for controlling it.* The CFO should question and control the number of *anything*, including the number of chairs to be ordered. That may seem extreme to many a CEO, but it serves a purpose. It is the ultimate control over rampant spending or uncoordinated purchasing.

Looking at it that way, there is a check and balance for all departments and individuals ordering materials of any size that affect the cash position and profitability of the company. Further, the CFO should speak up in executive meetings and when invited into board meetings, making sure that any major issues are vetted by the group.

I was an early angel board member of a company that subsequently raised over $30 million in venture money following the angel rounds, which themselves amounted to $6 million. I remained on the board through the life of the corporation, a witness to some surprises along the way that were, at the least, instructional. First, the VC's ordered that the company ramp its burn rate (monthly losses in cash) to over $800,000, which I could not fathom. But it was their money and they must know what they were doing, I thought, as I watched what I thought to be all-or-nothing spending. The CFO dutifully followed the VC commands to spend, and managed the spending process well – even if it exceeded reasonable standards of control over the ever-increasing inventory, headcount, and fixed expenses as the infrastructure grew.

But the CFO let the spending rate continue to increase out of balance with the board-approved budget which projected revenues to ramp, reducing the monthly cash burn. In one four hour board meeting with all in attendance, the board spent almost an hour with the CFO analyzing the financial performance of the company. We never saw, and he never mentioned the balance sheet and cash position. It was eight months after the latest $11 million round and no-one thought it worth focusing on cash, since the position should have been over $5 million in cash and starting to grow - if on plan.

A week after the board meeting, the CFO emailed the board that the company was only weeks from having no cash in the bank. Can you guess the board's reaction? The CFO was immediately fired. I performed a forensic audit on behalf of the board to determine if there had been any fraud or theft; but there had been none. Spending had continued out of control, much of it for inventory and assets - neither of which appear on the income statement. So those expenditures were not reviewed by the board which had not been given a balance sheet to examine.

The moral is simple. A CFO is responsible for all phases of cash deployment and preservation. Failure to manage to plan, and failure to inform the board of dangerous excursions, caused this company to fail as the VC's decided ultimately not to continue to pour money into the investment.

Maybe the CFO could not have saved this company; but he surely could have slowed the flow of cash, informing the board, and giving the board and CEO the opportunity to pivot the plan, to reduce inventory, to reduce spending, or to consider looking for a strategic partner or buyer.

Especially in companies where the CEO or founder is not a financial expert, the CFO is expected to be knowledgeable, willing to confront as well as inform, and to find early warning metrics that help in the process of effective cash management. That person is not a bookkeeper, counting the past, but an expert at forecasting and control.

Be an Adaptive Business Leader.

The title of this insight happens to be the name of a CEO roundtable organization I belong to, and have been a member since 1989 (Adaptive Business Leader Organization – or ABL). The organization, like Vistage, manages roundtables of CEOs meeting monthly in small groups, where they discuss their mutual challenges and help solve each other's complex problems, acting as an informal board of advisors. Unlike other groups, ABL members all belong to either healthcare or technology industry-focused roundtables. There they not only discuss their business issues, but significant business-changing trends facing their industry. Since I am chairman of the Technology side of the Organization, I attend more than one ABL group each month, and estimate that I've now attended more than four hundred half-day roundtables over the years.

Why would I spend so much time networking with other CEOs, discussing mutual problems and solutions? The answer is that I am the recipient of many insights from fellow CEOs that sometimes strike like lightning bolts when least expected. It was an Internet CEO roundtable in early 2000 where it became obvious before the public was aware, that the bubble was just beginning to burst for such tech businesses. And it happened again in early 2008, as CEOs reported the first evidence of order slowdowns and issues with customer payments – right before the 'great recession.'

But most importantly, it is the constant hearing of stories by these CEOs of how they were able to adapt to changes in their environment and alter the course of their leadership, adapting to external influences that had changed in their industry or the economy.

At each session we hear one of the dozen or so members present in depth, requesting feedback from each member of the group in response to a list of concerns that is explained during the presentation as background for the help hoped for from the group. I contribute my two cents of advice, as do the others in the group. As an active, professional angel investor, often I can help in areas not familiar to the others, when fundraising issues are on the list.

There's the story of the member-CEO who saved her company during the great recession by dismantling its fixed overhead, sending everyone home to work virtually, and building a new culture to successfully support over one hundred workers from home. Her recruiting business survived and flourished even as others closed their doors during the recession - and have remained shuttered.

Ten years ago, a young entrepreneur joined one of the roundtables, and we followed his progress with his issues, many of them directly related to fundraising, as he grew his company from a raw start-up to an initial public offering on the NASDAQ exchange, followed by continued growth in revenues and stock price. During the early years, he often asked for advice about funding, comparing various sources and offers, threading the needle between the wishes of the investors and his judgment as to how to grow the company.

Somewhere along the way, as he grew his company to a size larger than any others around the table had ever managed, we became the students, listening to a set of concerns that were often stunningly beyond any we had experienced. With a small stake in his company, and monthly contact through these roundtables, I happily find myself the former teacher, now the student.

The theme of these roundtables is "adapt" – to be ready for and embrace change quickly and efficiently in the light of opportunities and changes that might be missed by other CEOs without trained antenna-like skills.

You, too, can be an adaptive business leader, if you spend time with your ear and nose to the ground, listening and looking for signs of opportunity and change, then acting quickly to accommodate or take advantage of limited windows in time. It is a skill that can be taught. More importantly it is one requiring that you spend some amount of your time looking for signs of change. Many of us are locked in the daily grind of our business, and default to managing events and reacting to incoming stimuli, such as emails and internal requests for assistance.

An adaptive leader seeks out change and embraces the opportunity to take advantage of trends early in their cycle, or to reconstruct a business in response to early signs of trouble or weakness.

Start by paying more attention to indicators of change within and outside your organization. Gather information to support your observations. Then act when appropriate to secure the advantage or protect the enterprise.

Seek out a roundtable organization if you can, to find a group of fellow executives ready to share and solve your problems of the month, or share theirs with you to better inform you of those you might otherwise miss in your management life. It is certainly worth the time and effort to hone your skills at becoming an adaptive business leader.

You may burn your first professional manager.

It seems to be a rule, not an exception. The first professional senior manager that an entrepreneur hires to share the growing workload does not last more than a year.   Why?

Entrepreneurs start businesses with a strong vision of *what and how*, involved in every process from buying supplies to hiring and directly supervising early employees. The culture of the company is built day by day by those actions, often centering on the founder's vision and management style with little room for deviation.

At some point, as the company grows, either the founder's span of control is stretched to the limit, or investors enter the picture, often with a clear idea of how they would like to scale the company to grow quickly. This happens predictably, either voluntarily in the case of the founder deciding that s/he needs help at or near the top, or involuntarily when investors insist upon the addition of professional leadership.

If this new executive hire is the first for a founder or founding partners, and if the person is expected to relieve some portion of the that executive workload, there is a predictable and great risk that the first person hired to do so will last only a short time at the company.

I've seen this happen so many times, it is almost a rule for me. I warn the entrepreneur to be careful in the interview process, to expose the candidate to people at all levels of the company for buy-in, to be absolutely sure that there is a culture fit. But most important of all, I warn the founder that s/he must be ready and able to let go, to delegate clearly, and to establish metrics for measuring the performance of the newly hired executive – but not to interfere with that person's day to day management unless absolutely necessary. I urge the founder to coach, but not to expect the new executive to be a duplicate in style or perceived ability.

It is an unhappy but common occurrence: the recently hired and trained professional manager is let go, and a new search started. Luckily, in my experience, the second person hired for the job often is much more successful – usually not because the person is better at the job, but because the founder is more willing to delegate, expecting less a duplication of self.

If this is so common, is it not possible to be aware of the probability, and condition yourself to be more tolerant of someone else's different style of leadership? It might be a learning opportunity for the founder, often coming from one more experienced in the position and in growing company leadership.

Hire slowly. Fire fast.

New hires can shore up the weak areas of a business in ways existing employees cannot, if hiring is done to fill true needs. Some employees lose their drive, or remain behind as the company grows, failing to gain the experience or knowledge needed to manage expanded processes or numbers of subordinates. Sometimes, there is just too much work for one person, and a second is needed to continue growth. And of course sometimes, a person leaves the company, creating a need to fill a hole.

There is a rule few follow. Slow down and take more care in the hiring process. Vet the candidates well, even though you think that you do not have time enough to do so. Hiring is one of your most important duties, a way to increase the quality and productivity of your company's staff.

Every hiring opportunity is a window to improve the company. Hire slowly, with the weight of that opportunity clearly in mind.

On the other hand, we are all guilty of hanging on to marginal employees for too long. It is humane; it is easier to do nothing. It is less of a drag on your time to let marginal employees continue to plug along in their job. We have all done this. And yet, we have all looked back after a painful separation of a marginal employee, and thought that we should have made the move to replace the person much earlier. We agree that the person would have benefited with a better fit, and the company would have surely performed better having hired the replacement earlier.

It is human nature to hire as quickly as possible, to reduce the time taken from a busy day for interviews and reference checking. And it is human nature to hang on to marginal employees. Both are opposite the best practices of good management.

Try to force yourself to slow down in the hiring process, and speed decisions you know will someday have to be made about marginal employees.

The five "Whys"

This is a trick headline. There can be three "whys" or twenty, depending upon the issue and the responses. To make the point, the word "why" has to be one of the more powerful words in a manager's vocabulary. Asking the question forces the other person to think beyond the usual "what" that generated a response to "why."

It sure is a way to get to the bottom of an issue. "I just reduced the number of ad words we're paying for." "Why?" "They weren't paying off in enough revenue." "Why?" "Well, all we could measure is dollars of revenue against cost for clicks." "Why?" "Well, we have no way to know which other ad words might have done a better job of conversion into revenue." "Why?" "We have no-one on staff with enough knowledge of marketing to distinguish words from phrases, or with experience to know how to capture clicks into conversions." "Why?" "We've never thought this to be an important part of our marketing effort." "Why?" "We just don't know what we don't know. Will you stop asking 'why'?"

How revealing! There is no better way to get to the bottom of an issue than this. In the case above, lack of performance was caused by lack of knowledge, and inability to find resources to help. A good manager-questioner might conclude that a small expenditure with a consultant might pay off in great rewards, before abandoning the use of ad words entirely as a result of the comment from the subordinate.

Practice your listening skills with one or more attempts at the five "why's" and see if you find insights into answers to problems that might not have been obvious without your queries.

Stay in touch with your investors.

Investors as a group have a common gripe - almost universal. Information flows from the company irregularly, in fact most often when the company is urgently in need of more money.

Investment documents usually call for quarterly reporting by the company to the investors. Less than a quarter of companies receiving early stage investment voluntarily fulfill this promise. Usually, one or more of the investors is placed on the board as a requirement of the investment documentation. The entrepreneur often expects that person to keep fellow investors informed. And sometimes the board member does perform the service. But most often, the CEO or founder has a much better idea of the flow of quarterly activity than a board member meeting monthly or less often, and for a relatively short period of time. More importantly, the investors want to hear directly from the CEO.

Many times, companies need another round of investment, and the first people approached are the same ones that invested the first time. If they have not been kept informed about the progress of the company, and if they are surprised by the fact that the company has run out of money more quickly than planned, it is a much harder sell to obtain the next round than the last.

Rob Wiltbank, Ph.D., of Willamette University, is one of several academics who have followed multiple rounds of investment in a significant group of early stage companies. The typical finding is that second round investments are not as profitable for the investor as the first round. So investors are more cautious as a result when approached for additional money if not kept in the loop between rounds. If a company is meeting milestones and growing as projected, and if the CEO is diligent in keeping the investors informed, a second round is much more likely to be raised from the early investors. But the studies include all second rounds, including those that were pulled from investors reluctantly to protect their first money in, skewing the curve away from more heavily weighting successful conclusions.

Keep your investors informed. Avoid late surprises. Plan financial needs early, and inform investors early of that plan. Explain problems encountered and solutions undertaken. You and they will benefit by this candor and communication.

You are watched more closely than you think.

Ever had a manager above you who said one thing and did another? At least once? Or in a pattern of repeats? Well, you're not alone. Did you think less of that person for it? Would you follow that manager to the ends of the earth? Well, almost everyone has had multiple such experiences with a senior manager. And most people think less of that person than before.

On the other hand, think of the professional you most admire. Do you know of any times that person has made promises to you and missed on delivering them? The difference comes down to trust and respect. We lose both when we catch someone, especially someone above us, acting differently than his or her self-proclaimed rules, or even violating company rules.

It is one of the most vital elements of good management – restraining oneself when rank would ordinarily grant special privilege, and instead acting as one would expect a subordinate to act.

Black and white examples include taking supplies home, using company time to perform personal duties (if not permitted), and even traveling business class at company expense on short trips. Larger and more important examples involve direct promises that are broken, such as review dates with implied raises, or promised follow-through on an issue of great urgency to person receiving the promise.

Everything you do as a manager is watched by one or many. The very culture of the enterprise is shaken when someone in power gets away with bending or breaking the rules expected to be adhered to by all. Why have rules, or a company handbook, or new employee orientation sessions if the actions don't match the words?

And once violated, it is almost impossible to retract the action. That should make us think twice before taking small liberties.

Do you tell your direct reports HOW to do a job?

Unless your job is to teach, attempting to tell your direct reports HOW to do the job you've asked or ordered them to do will be a disincentive, will remove some of the authority you've delegated, and definitely reduce their motivation to act and lead.

Think for a moment of sometime in the past where someone directed you to do a job, then launched into a lengthy explanation of how you should do it. How did you feel at that moment? I'd bet that you were either silently or openly angered that the person assumed that you didn't know how to do a job even before asking if you did. This has been true since we were kids, and dad told us to rake the leaves, and then launched into an explanation of what tools to use and how to do the job. If that happened to you in some form over the years, I'll bet you pushed back immediately with something like "I know how to do that, Dad." You felt diminished by dad's assumption that you didn't know how to do the job.

The same is true in business, even if there is less drama and far less confrontation exhibited by the respondent. It is perfectly logical for that person to ask for help, or to a lesser extent to immediately offer it without a request. But it is a grand disincentive and personal affront to force upon a respondent a short lecture on how to do a job without being asked.

Most of us would think that it is just good management to provide another tool – teaching how to complete the task when asking for it to be done. Not true. Remember dad's doing that to you years ago.

It is a lesson in understanding human pride and dignity. Don't include "how" when you tell a person "what" and "why," unless they ask for help.

Don't manage with "what" without "why!"

Empowering your direct reports with the reasons for your orders gives them incentive to act, motivation to accept authority, and purpose behind action. I try to teach this with the simple phrase that is the headline of this insight.

Think of the last time someone above you in your business or personal life gave you an order to do something that seemed either illogical or of low priority - to you. If you accepted the authority of the person giving you the order, you just performed the task, probably either wondering if that person was nuts or whether you just didn't understand the reason for the task.

What if that person had told you why it was important to be done, in clear terms that related to that person's priorities? Wouldn't you be more prepared to perform the task knowing the context?

I just spoke with an old friend who is in sales. He lamented the fact that his boss recently layered several more sales reports on him to complete each week, reducing his selling efficiency. How many times have we heard this complaint, especially from sales people? I suggested that he go back to his boss and explain that it would be more than just helpful to know why these new reports are needed, that even though the salesman has no need to know, it would certainly make doing the work less of a chore. And by the way, I offered, if the boss could not explain why, there might be an opening to advance the argument that the trade in time between completing the new report and reduced sales call time might be worth a revisit of the order.

How many tasks, reports, and rules hang around the necks of people throughout a more mature organization, which remain as "what" without anyone remembering "why?" It is probably as effective a tool for the manager as for the recipient of the order, to explain *why* when telling *what* to do.

Your employees will appreciate the small extra effort, better understand the reason behind the request, and perform the act with more enthusiasm. What's not to like about that?

Help your employees to grow through their position.

When we accept the work commitment from a person we hire, we make a pact with the new employee that often stops at agreeing to pay for service rendered and to provide a safe working environment.

There should be more than that. With some people you hire, you know you are just renting their services as they pass through your organization, aimed at a higher calling. Others want to know that they are signing on to a career, not a job, and expect to move up within the ranks or on to a larger company that can accommodate their goals.

A recent statistic I saw surprised me. But as I thought of examples of people I know, it seemed more accurate than I would have imagined. The average new college graduate today will work thirteen jobs in his or her career, in an average of five different fields. Ouch! What happened to a job for life? How can employers expect complete loyalty if there is no clear upward path to the top for the best new hire?

The answer coming from the best of breed in corporate personnel management is to form a trusted bond with that openly-identified employee, helping that person to manage his or her career within and preparing to follow the company experience. If a superstar agrees to work for you for a period while learning the ropes to move to a better job elsewhere, assuming that there is candor in the communication by the employee and a level of trust in and by the employer, it is perfectly proper to offer to help that employee succeed. The pact between employee and employer is that the employee gives the best possible service to the company, in return for the company helping the employee to grow in, and perhaps beyond the position.

Especially with young entrepreneurial CEOs, this feels to them like a stick up. "Give me your money, and I will work only until I find a better job." And that attitude might be warranted if the employee just performs to the minimum required level, marking time to the next opportunity. But if the person has skills and knowledge that the company needs, there is the basis for a fair trade of talent and time for a later organized, positive move to the next level outside of the company.

With that openly positive corporate attitude, you can celebrate the growth of the employee with a party as the person graduates, instead of either feeling anger when an employee resigns with short notice, or being suspicious that the employee will leave with trade secrets in tow. Certainly other employees will see the supportive behavior, understand the company's contribution to the career of this upwardly mobile employee, and celebrate not only the graduation event but the great culture of the company itself.

Are you too emotionally involved in the decision?

Negotiating an agreement, especially one that involves personal gain, is tough for the person personally involved. There is too much to lose to be objective, to be willing to walk when terms go upside down.

It is my experience that you should have an expert negotiator with you or even in your place, whether from your board or an employee or outside professional such as an attorney – when the issue is personal.

Think of buying a car, for example. If you are looking for your spouse or offspring, it is probable that they've picked out the perfect car and are ready to take it off the dealer's hands. Assuming that you are the elected as or self-assigned to be the negotiator, the last thing you want is to have them in the room while you haggle over price. Advantage other side.

Negotiating on behalf of business associates too personally involved in a transaction: it's a role I've played tens of times over the years. There are the several that were disengagements between partners threatening to sue each other for perceived wrongs. There's the sale of a company, where as a board member, I asked the CEO to name his asking price and then go home and wait the result. There's the disengagement with an angry employee threating to sue the company.

All of these are personal issues to a CEO or founder or entrepreneur. And all of them draw that person emotionally into making decisions that cannot easily be objective, or into finding solutions that are mutually acceptable without the torture of constant re-explanation of opposing positions.

A smart lawyer, they say, should never represent himself. And yet, lawyers are trained in the art of negotiation. You should be careful not to miss the point of that admonition.

My oldest son learned to accompany me, but keep a deadpan look on his face as I negotiated for his ideal car, completing the purchase in minutes. The CEO described above endorsed his company selling for twice his asking price, after his absence helped the negotiation to be completed within an hour. The partnership described above dissolved without suit after a personal visit by the negotiator without the first partner present resulted in settlement within an hour. The employee just described accepted a severance check in trade for a release, without the emotion of arguing out old issues between employee and employer.

Are you too emotionally involved in a decision? Consider the advice lawyers give each other, and find a surrogate to argue your case.

Fire yourself. Rehire a new you.

When a new CEO or manager is hired into a company, for a while lots of energy flows from the top and new ideas seem to be generated daily. It is one reason not to fear the unknown when upper level management long in place turns over, often leaving most everyone worried about the future of the company and for their own prospects.

Even the best of us fall into a routine in our jobs. It is human nature to do so, but it is not a sign of our best efforts. We recall the enthusiasm we had for the job earlier, how we couldn't wait to get to work, or initiate a new plan, or share a new idea. We can be that person again. It just takes a bit of effort to change our mindset.

We may run out of fresh ideas after a time; most of us do. But there are sources of great ideas right next to us in our own company, or available to us from fellow CEOs, or from industry consultants with a broader view of the landscape, uninhibited by our need to meet daily obligations.

One of my most respected CEOs arrived at his monthly CEO roundtable meeting years ago and announced that he had just fired himself. He had reconfigured the company, delegating many of his previous responsibilities, and rehired himself in a new position more strategic to the company, retaining the CEO title. It was an attitude adjustment, self-initiated. He credits that effort as the start of his company's real growth, resulting in a great public company, dominant in his field.

Another CEO described how he drove to work each Monday morning forcing himself to think of what he would do if he were a newly hired CEO, fresh on the job that day. He surprised himself with his many fresh ideas, just with that change of perspective.

However you do it, refresh yourself. Be that new CEO - but with all the knowledge and skills you already have as a head start.

Protect your outlier innovators.

Here's one for executives of technology companies, or any company with next generation products in mind. As your business grows more complex and there are more employees to manage and more customers to care for, slowly you will notice that more and more time of your chief innovation officer or system architect or R&D department is spent focused upon enhancements in response to needs of the user base.

The company's most valuable technical visionary, the person tasked with staying out in front of new technologies, developing the next generation of new products, and thinking "a mile above the box" is drawn into working on projects that are incremental to the product and to the existing business. Often he or she will approach you and state that the work has become more boring, and that there is no time left for creative thinking or next generation experimentation and development.

That's one scenario. In many companies, there are people who are quiet geniuses, wanting to work on projects outside of the daily focus of the department or company. Managers sometimes view this behavior as non-strategic or wasteful, and even sometimes will isolate or reject these outside thinkers outright.

Or finally, you may want to start a project using the next generation of tools to produce an entirely new product – but your development resources are all tied up with projects to enhance existing products. Whichever of the three scenarios may apply to you, it is a red flag for your future if you condone the status quo, and allow the company to devote all of its resources to existing products and simple enhancements. Your best creative thinkers will leave you, looking for more challenges than you can offer. Your competitors may already be working on the next generation of product, as you remain stuck in the mud, even if focused upon serving the customer base with outstanding service and rapid feature rollout.

It is up to you to decide if research and development for advanced or next generation products is a strategic priority for you and your company. If so, you have a duty to protect these future-focused developers or architects, removing or reducing the pressure of reactionary development work, and isolating them in a space that prevents constant interruption by others focused upon day-to-day work.

Technology companies are prime targets for this problem. Every six to ten years, there is an entirely new platform to focus upon for the next generation of products. Just think of the computer and software fields. First there were mainframes, followed by minicomputers, then client-server systems, then peer-to-peer networks, then the Internet, mobile devices, cloud computing, and now mesh networks. Each generation required new tools, rewrites of software, creation of new user interfaces.

And in each generation, there are dominant players from the past generation that fade as new companies not inhibited by the demands of their user base leap beyond the last generation's leaders with new systems for the new age. Leaders of significant size are sometimes made irrelevant over time, or pivot into service organizations, or absorbed into growing next generation companies.

What happened to Wang, Sperry-Univac, Burroughs-Unisys, DEC, RCA, and hundreds of early generation leaders? Their CEOs did not provide enough of a safe environment and enough resources to their creative geniuses to make the leap into that next generation.

It is a cost of doing business that you cannot ignore. Not only providing resources for next generation development, but protecting the people performing those development tasks should be one of your strategic priorities.

A tale of two CEOs and the management of pain

This is the tale of two CEOs, one of them unfortunately....me. It's a story of how people handle unusual situations when selling to the top – an executive of a prospective customer. And the stories couldn't be more different.

Recently a CEO friend told me her story of a dinner with her director of business development and an executive of a major company, a candidate for a large sale. As the dinner progressed, he started, and then continued to excuse himself from the table, looking paler each time. After several of these, upon his return, she asked him if everything was OK. He responded, like most of us would, that all was OK, and that he was having a bit of trouble breathing, would probably have to leave the dinner early, and drive home.

She took one more look, and went into decision mode. "No, you aren't fine," she stated. "Give me your car keys; we're going to the hospital." He reluctantly acquiesced, and she tended to him as her director drove all three to the hospital. She had him call his wife on the way to meet them at the hospital. As they waited in the emergency room, after more episodes, his breathing finally became easier, and by the time the doctor saw them, he could find nothing of worry, ruling out stroke or heart attack. Our CEO then returned to the restaurant and met with the chef to have him list all the ingredients from the meal the executive was eating. The problem was, as you guessed, an undiscovered food allergy, with a possible ambulance ride averted and a happy ending. The executive even tells the story now that the CEO may have saved his life, because he was unwilling to own up to the fact that his breathing was so very difficult.

Now, I would not have been so fast to take charge. Maybe it's a guy thing. I would have been thinking about the sales relationship and the sale, and would probably have let the guy drive home, acknowledging his discomfort, and ending the dinner early.

This leads me to my story. Years ago, I was in the process of selling a $125,000 system to a well-known baseball hero who owned his namesake hotel in St. Louis. Flying on the red eye to make a morning appointment, his hotel bus driver dropped me off in the dark a few feet beyond the lighted portico. I stepped off the van into... a recently dug pit about two feet deep, and broke my foot in the fall. What pain! I tried to sleep in the room they gave me, and managed to make it to the 10:00 AM meeting with the very well-known sports figure and sales candidate. He saw me drag my leg into the conference room, made no comment, but asked if I would like a tour of the hotel. "Of course," I said, ignoring the pain and dragging my foot the entire way through the tour.

Well, I didn't make the sale. And I didn't sue the hotel. I was in selling mode and nothing was going to detract from my focus or reputation.

I sure was not admitting to the problem or seeking recourse for the obvious flagrant error by the hotel in not marking the excavation.

Who was right? Well, I should have led the meeting with my story of woe in order to protect others. The other CEO took charge, and made a friend of both the potential customer and his spouse, who she called as they drove to the hospital.

Is it a guy thing? Is it conditioning us to put things in perspective regardless of the personal outcome, including a lost sale? I think about these two examples now, and have concluded that there are some traits of a great CEO that cannot be learned easily. Putting others above self, and sacrificing a short term goal is not easy for a type 'A' driven entrepreneur when the stakes are high. *But it is the right thing to do.*

Power is sometimes assumed when not granted.

How many times have you heard someone say "Let's do it now and ask permission later?" It's a common practice in companies where there is a barrier between levels in the chain of command, or lack of communication between contemporaries. The statement represents a failing at some point in the delegation or communication chain by a higher level of management, and should be taken as a warning that there is a problem greater than the issue handled at the moment.

I've worked with organizations that are so large that extensive paperwork is required to obtain approvals to accept customer orders, make any purchases of any size, or any commitment of resources. In every case, people try to stretch those restrictions in as many ways as possible to get around the time taken to complete forms and lost in waiting for approvals. It's the "order prevention department" syndrome.

Incomplete delegation of responsibilities, or controls that are too tight, both lead to a rationale for subordinates to circumvent the system.

The worst thing about this is that the people most likely to do this are those most entrepreneurial and creative in doing their jobs. Conversely, those most likely to fall back and seek guidance, clarification and direction are those most subservient and least creative.

Middle managers sometimes identify those who assume power as non-conformists or even troublemakers. It is rare to ever see a dialog come out of such an event that leads to better defined delegation of responsibilities, removal of roadblocks, or relaxation of overly restrictive rules. More often such actions lead to reprimands without analysis of the underlying general cause. And occasionally, the very creative, driven individuals you would otherwise celebrate are made candidates for elimination instead of catalysts for change.

Reward success and failure. Punish only inaction.

Reward failure? That may be a difficult concept for an executive. And there are limits of course. We wouldn't reward a failure to follow laws, or protect lives, or deliberate endangerment of the company or its people.

But should we reward a research team that fails for the fourth time to find the solution to a nagging problem - on the way to a new product? What if those failures are commonplace? Where do we draw the line? Edison tried a thousand types of material before finding tungsten for the core of the light bulb. If he had been a research employee reporting to you, at what point would you have pulled the plug on the project, or become disillusioned with the person?

The culture of the company you grow is very much influenced by your actions in rewarding or punishing employees or whole departments. And the best companies seem to be those that are motivated from the top to push limits within reason in order to find better ways to do things, to create products, to expand the market. The CEO must realize that most such efforts lead to a dead end or will fail outright.

I was once in the record business. Speak about insanity. Only two percent of all records released broke even. Of course, the major hits paid for thousands of misses. In venture capital, the conventional wisdom is that one in ten investments will more than pay for the complete loss of half of those ten investments. Yet investors reward the VC's with a track record of one in ten, and record companies still churn out a reduced number of recordings, knowing that a great majority will fail to break even.

So, where does the learned, best of breed CEO step in to administer punishment? As the headline infers, a visionary, proactive leader should not be able to stand by and condone inaction. That is not only a waste of corporate assets, but the fixed overhead eaten by the inactive period keeps draining the cash and time resources of the corporation with nothing to show for it. Wouldn't you rather dissect a failure and move forward, than have nothing to show for time and money spent in wasted fixed overhead?

The coffee and wine school of innovation.

Here's one for debate around a cup of coffee or a glass of wine. Most innovation occurs when creative people are relaxed and thinking about other things.

We all can picture the corporate R&D lab with tens of scientists working at white boards, or over computer models, or with prototypes. And we picture programmers working at their workstations or on their portable notebooks creating great new code.

But all of those people are following the flash of inspiration that started their activity, and it is that flash we seek to reproduce again and again in a successful enterprise.

This leads us back to coffee and wine, and showers, and quiet time. Given that we are looking for that flash of inspiration that starts us down the path of innovation through the hard work of R&D, maybe we should reengineer our thinking about allocation of time for our most creative resources, including ourselves.

There are times when creativity comes under pressure. Necessity, after all, is the mother of invention. But whole leaps into new groundbreaking areas of innovation most often come from times of reflection, when the mind is clear to dream ahead, to think without interruption.

So there are those who subscribe to the coffee and wine school, and encourage creative thinkers to find extra time in the early mornings or evenings to free the mind to innovate, to find the spark that could propel a company forward.

Protect your international traveling employees.

As your company grows, you will probably have to make conclusions about traveling employees, and travel for yourself. There are vast opportunities internationally that require careful planning to execute well. One of the most critical decisions is how to enter a new country or region. Most companies early in to the process do not have the resources to place people on the ground in foreign countries, so they make new relationships with distributors or dealers to represent them in the new areas.

As you begin your travels into new territories away from home, it is always wise to have a host to greet you from arrival through departure in each country that is new to you. If you do not yet have any firm relationships in a country, develop some connection using your outreach channels before the first flight. Even if you are going to start a series of interviews, you can have one candidate meet you at the airport and another later return you to the airport. You should find this connection occurs automatically later as the relationships mature and you have either dealers or your own personnel within each territory.

The customs, laws and even the knowledge of safety dos and don'ts are critical elements in assuring your safety and that of your traveling employees. It is also good business to learn local customs from locals. Having a local contact to provide information to your home and your work is a relief to all, including yourself.

Then there is the question of creation of a regional office to cover multiple countries in a geographic area. It is the next logical step toward creating corporate entities abroad. And the regional manager hired to oversee multiple countries can act as country manager for his or her home country, often volunteering to travel with you to the various countries in the region. That's the best and safest choice for a next step toward becoming a true, international entity with offices in numerous countries as you grow.

Money motivates.

Salaries or hourly wages must be within reasonable limits set by the industry and matched by the competition, both regionally and for the same job classification. But more difficult is the sticky issue of employee incentive compensation. I find that this is an area much more often the subject of a CEO phone call, a roundtable discussion, or a board compensation committee meeting.

There are many studies that can tell us how various industries reward employees for achievement above a base pay, or beyond expectation. And there are some industries where tools such as stock options are considered mandatory for a company to be competitive. But how about listing the basics for designing an excellent incentive compensation program? Here are several, gleaned from numerous companies and systems of compensation.

First, *be rule specific*. A bonus or commission that is granted after the fact, without a target plan or without objectives to meet, is surely appreciated, but does not often create an incentive to exceed, only an expectation of receipt again in the next period. When a leader and a subordinate agree upon a list of achievements in advance, then good performance can be rewarded based upon a fair assessment of accomplishments against those achievements. And if those goals are aligned with those of the overall corporation, everyone wins and the process can be repeated in subsequent periods.

Second, there should be a substantial carrot, or *upside bonus for outstanding achievement.* A sales commission plan should reward a salesperson with a combination of salary and commission up to the expected level of performance, often called a quota. Perhaps a part of that compensation plan should include a bonus upon achievement of quota, as a form of recognition and celebration. Then, contrary to popular thinking, there should be an increasing reward for achievement above the expected number, beyond the list of agreed-upon incentives for non-commissioned employees. For a salesperson, the commission percentage should increase above quota, and a second level of bonus available at some higher point. Sometimes, a combination of revenue, gross profit and even operating income form the basis for individual and team rewards.

Next, some form of rewards should be designed to *be immediate.* Rewarding a February achievement in December disconnects the reward from the event, reducing the effect of the reward itself. If we believe that money does motivate, then we should reward positive behavior immediately to reinforce that behavior.

Finally, and perhaps most difficult to design, there must be *protection against workarounds* or from employees gaming the system. Reward only gross revenues, and salespeople will push the limit of profitability, impacting the corporation but not their commissions. Real estate agents are paid as a percentage of the sale, not upon its relationship to the asking price. Sometimes, agents push their clients to accept low offers to assure a quick closing of a deal, since their participation percentage is only slightly affected by a price cut to close the deal quickly.

There are more insidious ways to game a compensation system. Wall Street brokers helped to create the financial crisis by following a bonus system driven by quantity, not quality of trades. Salespeople paid entirely upon closing a deal will care less about the subsequent completion of a complex, time-consuming transaction. Support people paid based upon the number of tickets closed will rush to close tickets at the expense of quality service. There must be thousands of such examples where poorly designed systems allow employees to achieve personal goals that are at odds with the best interest of the corporation or its customers.

So use these four items as a checklist as you create compensation plans for various levels and types of employees. *Rule specific; substantial upside bonus; immediate rewards; protection against working around the system.*

Two very powerful words: Great job!

The best managers we all know are the ones who take the time to praise good work in public, before an employee's peers. Most of us have a monthly award for the top person in a group of employees. And if we are big enough to formalize the process in a regular meeting, we make it a regular part of that meeting.

If you haven't already discovered this fact, such a process quickly becomes routine and predicable. Small companies have trouble finding new people to honor after a while. Some employees even disingenuously consider the process an exercise in pandering, discounting the effectiveness of the award, and disenchanting those very managers who thought they were reaching out to do a good thing.

For all of us, we should remember that the best possible way to honor great work is to do so immediately. A "Great job!" coming at the right moment from the boss is valued as an honest recognition of good work, especially if done in front of an employee's peers.

At times, it is an entire team that deserves the recognition, again immediately after doing a great job. I found a formula that worked for me where most of the employees were in several buildings on the same campus. First arranging for my assistant to obtain the appropriate amount of hundred dollar bills from the bank, and then to follow me around checking off names, I had my own personal holiday celebrating each individual in the team with a handshake, words of thanks, and a C-note. With lots of laughter and thanks, the celebration and words "Great Job" made for a completely memorable event. And those pop-up thank you visits from the boss certainly contributed to the culture of the company. Word does travel.

Remember to reward those not present at the moment, and remember that the amount should be grossed up to take care of taxes and be entered onto the payrolls of the employees so rewarded.

I'm sure you have your own way to making "Good job!" work for you and your team.

Some great coaches are younger than you are.

Especially for social media-based businesses, we all need to recalibrate our thinking about who is the teacher and who is the student. There is nothing wrong with a manager slowing a conversation to ask for more background when speaking to an often-younger and more involved associate. You know what I mean... The conversation goes something like this: "We found it on x site and using y app with z as our data object."

First, managers could not be paid enough or have enough time to stay entirely current with all of the details each employee or associate deals with daily. Yet, many times that other person tries to explain an important finding or breakthrough, or make a significant comparison, using names of destination sites or apps or tools we have never used or heard of.

Yes, age often has something to do with it. And occasionally, a manager has to work to join the club by trying new things, learning new tasks and using new language to relate to those already in the know.

I recall vividly one such experience. I helped to found an Internet game company, playing the role of founding investor, chairman and even temporary CFO. The company was destined to grow into a large, very valuable enterprise that we sold for many, many times our investment. But that first day with the new employees was a test for me. Many years older than any of them, their initiation was to insist that I spend no less than forty-five minutes playing for the first time first person shooter games against Internet-based foes. I had to acknowledge the difficulty of achieving high degrees of skill, and the size and terminology of the extended gamer community. But most of all, I had to gain acceptance as "one of us" in an environment where my CEO coaching and my money did not count.

That was a lesson for me. Taking the time to be taught by those able to master a skill or have extra knowledge is an important step to show respect for everyone at all levels in an organization. And that respect flows in both directions, worth so much more than the time it takes to learn a skill or terminology or meaning.

Stealing time

It's a big issue within any company. With easy access to Internet shopping, games, social networks and more, employees are able to find many ways to focus on personal issues while at work, detracting from productivity and demonstrating a dis-respect for the time paid for by their employer. In fact, if we were to be direct, we might label it "stealing time," and consider it a crime of sorts.

Based upon the actual "loaded" cost of an employee per hour, that is certainly not an insignificant cost for the employer. Certainly it amounts to many times the cost of stealing something tangible, such as a ream of paper from the supplies cabinet. Yet, many of us treat the latter much more severely than the former.

Let's consider counter arguments. Attracting great employees often requires us to offer special incentives, including flexible hours, unsupervised time off, and access to perks such as free food and soft drinks. Often, employees just expect some degree of freedom when they work, to be able to quickly shop or communicate with friends in the middle of their day. In times past, older generations were perhaps more discrete when making personal phone calls (how ancient this sounds). But they often did so anyway, and often spending more time and more company money in phone bills than today's typical employee distraction.

How about the counter to the counter argument? There is no way to sugar-coat the fact that paid time is for work, not for outside play. The cost may seem small until someone calculates the combined cost over a year of time and screams "thief!"

As in all two-sided arguments, there usually is a middle ground. The boss who requires complete adherence to the work-every-minute ethic called for in the employee handbook generates ill will when enforcing the rule. But the manager, who openly ignores the behavior, encourages more of it from employees who will fall in to follow the example they see openly acknowledged.

My solution is to acknowledge the fact of life, equate it to personal time once used for personal calls, and define a 'limits of acceptability' publicly. "We recognize how difficult and intense your work is. We think it prudent for you to take breaks as often as every hour if you need them. We expect your breaks to be self-policed and no longer than ten minutes, to be used for all personal issues including personal use of your workstation. Remember not to stray out of bounds of corporate decency and confidentiality, and be safe in protecting corporate security."

Extending Your Runway

Several years ago, I wrote a book entitled, *Extending the Runway*, using parallels to piloting a plane to equate to the process of creating and building a small company, making maximum use of resources to get to and beyond breakeven. It is worth revisiting the most important point of that book, which was written to prompt discussion between entrepreneurs, professional managers and their boards of directors about issues that could unite them or strain the relationships between them.

There are five types of resources a great board can add to a company. These are: *time, money, relationships, context and process*.

Time: The longer it takes to produce and release a product, the more fixed overhead is consumed, and the runway of remaining cash diminishes. Expert help and good planning can reduce the time to market, saving cash in the process.

Money: A board of directors is primarily responsible for oversight in the use of and the raising of money for the company. There is a fine line between loading the company with too much debt, and diluting the shareholders too early with additional equity investments. But all agree that a good board will express its stewardship well by preventing the company from running out of money.

Relationships: One reason for having an effective board is to give the CEO a resource for tapping into great relationships that are owned by the various board members, so that the CEO can reach out and find help in areas most needed. If a board member has few appropriate relationships in his or her field of expertise or from past experience, then perhaps the board member is not appropriate for the company at this time. And if the board member refuses to volunteer or allow such relationships when needed by the CEO, that board member should be held to task by the other members of the board.

Context: Every good board has recruited at least one industry expert, often as the fifth or mutually-approved outside member. With expertise in the company's industry, that person can and should provide expert advice about the timing of the company's product entrance and applicability in the industry it addresses. A great product at the wrong time or a poor product unable to address the needs of the industry will fail in the marketplace. That board member should be actively involved in questioning the positioning, marketing and even the design of the product to avoid just such a disaster.

Process: Here, most experienced board members can help to streamline the process of product development, manufacture, channel management and marketing. Knowing how to scale from test to release or how to complete a process more quickly saves money and time, making this knowledge as valuable as raising more money for the company, but without the cost in dilution or debt.

Use your board to help you to navigate through control over these five resources. If you don't have a viable, relevant board, build one no matter what your size and stage of development. One thing is usually sure: an entrepreneur cannot successfully do it all alone.

It's about time.

While we are revisiting the issues raised by my earlier book, *Extending the Runway*, we should examine the challenges to a CEO in making use of enterprise time, one of its most valuable and often misused assets. Enterprise time, as opposed to personal time management, is defined as the sum total of resources available to a company expressed in terms of time – time to develop, to debug, to produce, to deploy, to respond to issues, and to make changes in plans that are not working.

By reducing the amount of time to perform any of these actions, the company saves fixed overhead and increases profit or reduces cash burn. So this issue becomes one to be dealt with by every manager at every level of the organization. Building efficiency into every corporate activity should be a corporate mandate, one to be discussed interdepartmentally, to be refereed by the CEO.

There is the flip side to making efficient use of time. I've labeled this *time bankruptcy* to make the point as dramatically as possible that this is a critical, company-threatening sinkhole that must be avoided at all costs.

Time bankruptcy is the ultimate result of the deliberate over-commitment of a company's most valuable resource(s) by the CEO or a department leader. There are many ways to fall into this trap. But the first thing to do is to identify what those critical resources are in your company. Most often it is the time of the chief architect of the product or service you provide, or of the best developers of that product. Sometimes it is the time of the CEO, which when overcommitted, prevents others from gaining access to solve critical problems or continue the flow of production.

One way to fall into the time bankruptcy trap is to release a product too early, and pay the price by forcing the architect and most skilled developers to drop off of their important tasks to put out fires in the field and fix problems one at a time.

Another is to fail to complete a contracted service for one customer and to do so multiple times, until many customers begin screaming for attention, drawing away all available talent from new, income earning tasks.

You will surely be able to identify an example of time bankruptcy that you have experienced in your past or present. It is your job to drive the company out of the time bankruptcy zone and to watch for signs of it occurring in the future, stopping the process before it becomes critical. That means watching quality control efforts more carefully, developing metrics to track incomplete processes and track remaining time committed to completion, watching the number of customers exposed to a new product or service before general release, and more.

It also means being careful that you, as a senior manager, do not become overloaded to the extent that you are unavailable or inefficient in helping those who need your attention to complete their tasks. Use the term, time bankruptcy, in a planning session, and see what response you get from your managers and employees. You'll be surprised at their understanding of the issue as it relates to their being able to complete their tasks successfully and of their contributions to solutions that will benefit everyone and increase process efficiencies.

Finally, enterprise time equates to available runway, or remaining cash and resources that you can call upon to gain market share and increase corporate value. Spending enterprise time inefficiently burns those resources unnecessarily. If you have enough reserves in cash and in time, you can dig out of the hole. But if you are managing a marginal business, the effective use of time as a resource extends your ability to make changes, reposition, react and build.

So if you wonder why we focus on this subject to the extent of seeming redundant, well then, *it's about time.*

Hire employees as if your survival depends upon it.
Aside from visionary management, this is your most important job.

Many of us go through the motions of hiring to fill a position, trying to use our intuition and skills to find the best candidate for the job. Sometimes we use consultants or recruiters; many times we use internal talent to fill most positions.

And over the years, we students of business success have learned that there is a science to the hiring process that continues through the life of an employee's tenure with the company. Bradford Smart captured this succinctly in his book, *Topgrading.* His thesis is that "A" players amount only to the top ten percent of the talent pool at any given time, and that your job is to find, recruit and retain only "A" players to make a successful business. It is hard to argue with that. What is hard to find, is the rare CEO that makes the process of hiring top recruits such a priority that he or she spends personal time deeply involved in the specification, resumé review, interview and selection of top employees. Most of us are "far too busy" to do all of that. And yet, aside from managing the vision of the enterprise, the most important job of a CEO is to find, recruit and make productive "A" players for the team.

As an investor and board member for numerous companies, it is increasingly easy for me to quickly evaluate the quality of senior team members in an organization as I probe for strengths and weaknesses in the enterprise. Teams where the CEO is comfortable enough to delegate to "A" players and manage the strategies for growth stand out as rare and powerful. Conversely, it takes very little for a CEO to derail what could be a great team and company, by ignoring the details involved in finding the right talent for each senior position, and by failing to communicate the strategies and empower the team to execute.

A successful hire is not just the responsibility of the recruiter and manager to whom the recruit will report. Many companies require that finalist candidates be interviewed by a number of contemporaries, good employees who fill similar level positions. Some even encourage interviews with those the candidate would manage. Agreement among the interviewers becomes an empowering experience for those conducting the interviews and agreeing to the decision to hire, and paves the way for a quicker assimilation of the new employee into the organization whose cohorts are already prepared to receive and encourage the new hire. This is not an inexpensive process when considering the cost in time and productivity of the interviewers. But finding "A" players is not an easy job, requiring a stretch of resources at each stage of the process.

Earlier, we explored strategic planning within the enterprise. We spoke of developing strategies and tactics that are measurable for each department. Now is a good time to complete that chain by suggesting that paying significant incentive compensation to the people empowered to execute those strategies and tactics is critical to the success of the plan as well as to the organization. Aligning everyone toward the same goal and using the practice of rewarding for achievement of milestones defined by the tactics from planning, makes for a great business, managed by a leader who understands the process.

What makes a great leader great? Of course, it's great execution by great employees acting as a unit in the best interests of the enterprise. No-one can do this alone. No CEO can do this with "B" players or less.

Fire fast, not last.

Here is one that takes a real leap for a younger manger or CEO to believe. After hiring someone with all of the attendant enthusiasm followed by the training and learning curve, if an employee shows signs of weakness in the job or problems dealing with contemporaries, it is the natural tendency for most of us to go first into coaching mode, and reset the observation clock to see if our excellent coaching does the job. A month or so later, when no apparent change has been noticed, we may move from coaching to a polite warning and maybe even the dreaded note-to-file. Another month, and the probability of a decision to separate becomes obvious and the move initiated. Lawyers will tell you that this progressive chain of moves is good for the company, protecting against lawsuits by a disgruntled former employee.

But surprisingly, in post-exit interviews after emotions have dissipated, most former employees (who were handled respectfully during the separation process) and most all managers will agree that the move should have been made sooner. The former employee will often state that he or she was at least somewhat unhappy in the job, knowing that the fit was not as good as it should be. The manager will most often admit that he did not move aggressively, following his best judgment in coaching the employee toward separation much earlier.

Firing fast in most every case is best for everyone, as opposed to long, drawn out sessions and stressful employee periods of waiting for a verdict in between sessions. It does sound counterintuitive. But I would believe the post-exit interviews. Why not conduct your own survey of fellow executives and managers and see what they think. If they agree, you should recalibrate your expectations and act sooner, all with the important caveat that employees must always be treated with respect, and there are many times when documentation to file is a required protection for the company against possible lawsuits, especially by protected classes of employees.

Equity is the currency of early stage businesses.

The truth of this statement may be obvious, but the execution of a good incentive program using equity is often mismanaged, damaging the corporate capitalization structure and even affecting the outcome of subsequent investment into the company.

First, a brand new enterprise is often formed from the efforts of several "partners", each with an expertise valued by the others. Equity is divided between the founders and the business begun. Although this insight does not address this point of ignition, we should note in passing that things always change over time, and formerly strong founder-contributors can become a drag upon a business or lose interest if the enterprise is not quickly successful. To protect against this, there must be some document in place from the beginning that clearly states the expectation of each founder as to contribution of time and resources to the enterprise. The document should also contain clear buy-sell clauses, forcing any sale of shares to first be offered to the corporate treasury, then to the other founders in proportion to their holdings, and then if no interest, to outside investors. It should contain a mandatory sale clause in the event of separation of a founder, so that a major owner who is passive in the enterprise cannot easily vote against measures other active founders endorse.

The real insight here is that stock options or phantom stock are the tools of early stage businesses used to attract great talent when there is not enough cash to pay market rates. There are some rules. First you must create a stock option plan using your attorney, which must be registered in many states as a security offering. (The fee for registration is well under $100, so this is not an issue.) Options are usually best with "C" corporations, but granting options for either LLC's or "S" corporations are not a real problem.

Most early stage companies make the mistake of making option grants to new hires at all levels that are too aggressive and distort the capital structure of the company to a degree that damages future professional investment. Let me try to advance a few rules of thumb to help guide you here. An option plan should carve out an addition of about 15% of the "fully diluted" shares. If there are 85,000 shares issued to the founders, then a plan calling for 15,000 shares in a pool reserved for future hires is appropriate, making the fully diluted shares 100,000. The board must approve the plan including this number, and shareholders must approve the plan as well. Each grant to new or existing employees must be approved by the board before issue.

The price per share for option grants is also an important consideration. IRS rule 409a specifically calls for an appraisal of the value of the corporation's stock current to within a year of any grants of options, although there is an exclusion for early stage businesses in which expert members of the organization or board may make such an appraisal if they qualify according to the exemption. If there is only one class of stock, the same as the founders, and the appraisal of the single class of shares yields, say $2.00 a share, then options must be priced at that amount. In other words, you cannot create bargain options at below "market rates." If you have a preferred class of stock with special protections, that class of shares will be valued at a price higher than the founder common shares, allowing stock options to carry a lower price per share than preferred investors may have paid. This is important because high quality candidates should be induced to consider coming aboard at lower than market salaries using the tool of "cheap" options, properly priced.

What percentage of the total company shares should be reserved for what specific job titles? Inducing a new CEO to come aboard usually means creation of a stock option package of 5-8%. That size of grant would take much or most of the option pool. A vice president, or CxO candidate, typically is offered between 1% and 1.5%. Director level employees are typically granted ½%. All other grants usually are much lower, allowing for the typical 15% pool to last for quite awhile in most companies.

We will cover board members and advisory board members at a later time.

Options typically are earned over time, which we call vesting. If a grant of 10,000 shares is made on January First, typically there is a four year vesting period in which the employee earns the right to exercise (buy) $1/48^{th}$ of the shares each month. Many plans also call for a one year "cliff" in which an employee who is separated from the company before a year is unable to exercise even the shares which would have been vested at that point.

There is an important consideration that will become an issue with sophisticated candidates for VP and above. We call these "trigger" provisions, in which selected options negotiated for a select group of senior managers, fully vest to 100% upon any change of control. This provision allows these select individuals to perhaps profit handsomely in an acquisition by being able to exercise their options in full at the time of sale. The negative side of this is that the buyer may not want to so enrich these managers that they may not be willing to come aboard the buyer's organization, even if the existing options are replaced with options from the buyer company.

If all of this seems a bit overwhelming, we have just scratched the surface of option plans and incentive compensation. This is an area of expertise that a CEO is required to quickly learn and carefully manage with the help of the corporate attorney and the board.

Align incentives with your goals.
And be generous to your high achievers.

Recently I was asked to review an offer letter for a senior director of business development. The CEO was concerned that he was offering far too much in the form of incentive compensation, with bonuses that could greatly exceed the base salary if all of the bonus items were achieved. I asked the CEO to imagine what the company would look like if all of those bonus-expensive items were completely achieved in one year. Upon reflection, he stated that revenues could double the following year, and that the company's reputation among larger customers would be so greatly enhanced that the company could become the leader in its niche. My obvious retort: "Then why not offer this candidate the moon if he can achieve this?" The offer was sent and the CEO was much happier, dreaming of the possibilities, not the incremental cost.

I love to point out that my top several sales people were making more than anyone else in the company, including their boss. These outstanding achievers worked for salaries below those of their engineering peers, and had to put it all on the line every day to earn their keep, let alone excel.

The best way to encourage alignment between your managers and the company's goals is to create a bonus plan for each, with its payments made based upon the key performance indicators established for them and for their areas of responsibility, all in turn based upon the tactics and strategies contained in the company's strategic plan.

It is amazing how few company CEOs grasp the concept that executives and managers should be compensated not just for doing their named job, but for exceeding expectations while advancing the corporate goals. To align everyone in the organization in exactly the same direction is a task, one that is a powerful driver for growth. People should be compensated well for such outstanding contributions.

What is the general rule for such a bonus plan? Provide no more than five key performance indicators derived from the strategic plan and fitted to the specific job of the manager. Set time-based goals for each. Provide bonus opportunities that add to approximately 50% of the base salary if all are achieved within the year. Meet and measure progress truthfully each quarter. Perhaps pay a portion of the bonus upon completion of these meetings. Do not make the usual mistake of ignoring or passing on the progress of any of these items by just paying a part of the bonus at yearend because no-one carefully reviewed progress, or because circumstances changed and the bonus item could not be completed as written.

Incentives are powerful tools when used well and reviewed often. They are a major part of a good manager's work and should be treated as such by the CEO and all senior managers.

Cash is only one measure of employee happiness.

In 1981, Herb Cohen wrote and published *"You Can Negotiate Anything"*, an excellent guide to great negotiating. I've read and reread the book a number of times and find myself using the techniques often in many areas of my life. One of his lessons remains clearly on my mind and is a variant of the old "You name the price and I'll name the terms" challenge that works so well in negotiation.

Cohen sets up an example where a senior position job candidate is stuck on a salary twice as high as the CEO is willing to pay, leading to a standoff between the two. Cohen goes on to point to twenty five non-cash items that the CEO could have used to narrow and eliminate the gap, many of them untaxed perks worth more than face value because of the employee's tax savings. They include an expense account, company car, profit sharing, 401k contributions, medical coverage for dependents, free life insurance, educational payments, extra vacation, relocation expenses, paid trips to industry association meetings, or a small override on revenue from new products developed under the candidate's watch.

One of the items on Cohen's list of twenty five was stock options. That of course jumps to the top of the list for young, fast growing technology companies. Many skilled, experienced executives have jumped from mature companies to more risky positions in smaller, fast growing enterprises primarily for the options. In a previous insight, we explored the common percentage of a company's fully diluted stock that is often granted in the form of options for new employees. (See insight 28.)

Many an executive has made much more than any cash compensation from exercise of "in the money" options after taking the leap to a smaller, fast growing company, attracted by just this form of incentive compensation. When used in combination with several of the twenty five additional non-cash forms suggested by Cohen, salary alone does not seem to be the barrier most people believe it to be.

Even a taste of ownership motivates employees.

How about employees all the way down the line and through the corporation? How do we align them to the goals and strategies of the enterprise? Obviously for the appropriate individuals, a bonus program aligned to the department's goals is appropriate. But how about awarding stock options for all employees?

I discovered the power of ownership early in my management career, establishing an employee stock ownership plan (ESOP), once popular as incentive compensation as well as a tax write-off for corporations and even a way to slowly transfer ownership of a company from the founders to the employees. These plans are not as popular today because of their complexity and difficulty to manage, lost in favor of simple stock option plans.

Each month, at the monthly company lunch for all, I'd greet everyone with "Hello shareholders", and proceed to show the assembled throng slides of high level financial statements, pointing out progress against plan. That form of open book management surprises many, but if the employees are stakeholders with a taste of equity, why not underscore the value of that equity by treating them as cohorts? Yes, sometimes the news is not good. They should know this, and from you not from the rumor mill. Your fear that the confidential information may get out to the industry competitors should be tempered by the fact that you are not giving out the secret sauce, just the results of the past period's performance. All public companies including your public competitors must do this in greater detail each quarter, and it rarely damages their ability to sell into the marketplace. Would bad news drive your best employees out the door?

Perhaps. But it is my experience with many companies that empowered employees, treated with respect and shared knowledge, will go far beyond expectation in remaining loyal to their associates and their employer.

And think of the time saved around the virtual water cooler if there are far fewer rumors to pass among your employees.

Review regularly. Act upon results.

Allowing small problems to escalate into big ones is simple. Just ignore the signs for long enough and the job is done. It takes far more energy to review regularly the key performance indicators you've established for each individual and yourself. But a small excursion caught early and corrected saves massive corrective resources later.

Take for example the manufacturing company with a small quality problem in one component, resulting in a test failure rate above the norm. You can just reject the components, especially if coming from an outside supplier, or you can get to the root of the problem by examining the cause and reengineering the process or product quickly, saving you and perhaps your supplier time and cost. Such a culture of quality engineering has an additional benefit in creating a higher bar for all to see, making the public statement that quality is a top priority.

The same careful management applies to virtually every person and process in the organization. If there are ways to measure successful output or execution, find them and use them regularly. If one person or department is not pulling its weight, others notice and if no action is taken, often others are discouraged because of the lack of management interest and control. The variant of "one bad apple" holds true in corporate cultures that to a degree entrepreneurial managers and young CEOs rarely credit – until a late correction is made and a collective sigh of relief can be heard company-wide.

Two most powerful words: "Help me."

Over the years I have heard many stories from entrepreneurs, students, news reporters, even my children, all telling me that they could not get someone's attention they wanted or needed until they used the words, "Help me." The simple request is disarming, enlarging the object of the request to a status of importance in respect to the questioner that is difficult to ignore.

There is a bit of the teacher in all of us, and a request for help is a natural trigger to bring this out. And there should be an equal - if not stronger - bit of a student in each of us as well, allowing us to drop our egos a notch and actually ask for help when we need it. There is no shame in admitting ignorance in even the most unusual of circumstances. Yes, this is true, even when we may think we know the answer in advance.

One of the many important tactics in negotiation is the strategic use of the words, "Help me," when attempting to understand the position of an adversary. Suddenly that person is in a position to explain the reasons behind a position, or facts that may not have been available to you, all in order to support his or her position. Armed with those new facts, a good negotiator can often craft a solution that addresses those concerns and achieves the goals of both parties.

Reporters and students learn this early when they attempt to get the attention of a busy CEO or politician. "I am a student studying your industry for a term report. Could you help me understand your issues so I can be sure to cover them in my research?" There are an untold number of doors opened and hours spent by very busy people in response to such simple outreaches asking "Help me."

Instead of hiding your ignorance about an issue in a discussion, a term used by someone on the other side of the table, a position taken by an emotional employee, stop and ask "Help me to understand."   I'll bet that nearly every time, the other person will pause and spend time teaching that would have been spent in persuasion.

How about asking for help when you do not know a process, the kind of help that might take hours or days of training, not just minutes of explanation? A busy person hearing this kind of request may respond with: "I know of a book" or "Here is a resource," or "Sure, you can sit in on our next training class." I have never heard an "I can't do that for you" in response to a "Help me" request.

And far beyond a simple technique in negotiation or attempt to access a busy executive, these two words are the key to lifelong learning. Who among us can't use that?

Hire for your core. Partner for the rest.

There is a major trend shaping up that is worldwide, already identified by hundreds of thousands of startup and small business CEO's. By carefully recognizing and focusing upon the very core of the business, these CEO's are allocating their scarce cash resources to hire the best talent they can find to support that core business, and then reaching out to partners, independent contractors, and other small businesses to provide all other functions.

There is much to reinforce in such behavior. By definition, your core is your intellectual property foundation, the thing that makes your business most valuable to customers, investors and perhaps someday to potential buyers. Every business has an intellectual foundation where the CEO's knowledge and vision create a barrier to entry that deflects some or much of the potential competition.

In the patent world, we protect this intellectual core with what we call a "patent thicket," aptly describing the attempt to surround the core patent with other patents that defend the core and further prevent competitors from attacking the central component of the business.

Sometimes we protect our core with effective branding and marketing. Or we do so with brilliant research and development, highly trained sales forces, large advertising campaigns, or secret processes.

Using this focused approach to hiring, companies can stretch their limited capital further, assure better protection of corporate secrets, and make use of the core skills of partners that are attractive and beyond the reach of a small company's abilities. In this new environment of cheap communication worldwide, it is only reasonable to leverage these advantages through partnering with those whose core complements yours.

Swarms, crowd sourcing, and tiger teams. Oh my.

As we grow our businesses, we inevitably run into problems that seem for a time impossible to overcome. Our development team is stumped with a problem; or the marketing organization cannot come up with a theme for the next campaign; or the team has hit a wall where further speed, size reduction, or other constraint seems impossible to overcome.

No one has the resources to solve all problems in all areas of the business. And every department can use creative thinking from others outside the department to overcome barriers created by "inside the box" thinking. There are at least three excellent methods of reaching out to solve seemingly insurmountable problems, aided greatly by virtual companies, cost-free distance communications and the newest mass communication tools such as group video conferencing.

First: *Swarming*. The project leader presents a problem to the entirety of the inside network of stakeholders, including suppliers and even customers if appropriate, and opens a channel for easy communication between the players. The group interacts quickly and solutions seem to fly in from several sides, tested and refined by the swarm until solved.

Crowd sourcing. Today, it is possible to easily send a problem out to the world of thinkers within and outside of our network, offering a reward in the form of money or prestige for the one solving the problem first or best. There is no fixed cost to this network-enabled technique until the solution is offered. And the sheer size of the open-ended workforce will create potential solutions far more creative than when the problem is presented to an internal group of departmental thinkers.

Tiger teams. No CEO wants to create a permanent team for a temporary problem. Most of us fear that such teams or committees find their own self-perpetuating reasons to continue after the primary problem has been solved. Tiger teams are formed with the specific purpose of focusing human resources upon a single problem, solving the problem then disbanding with a quick celebration of success. There is no issue of leadership succession, allocation of additional regular meeting time or even of failure. The team comes together to solve a single problem, and either solves it or passes it back for solving by an outside resource such as crowd sourcing if unable.

In each of these three methods of problem solving, the strength comes from the focus of a group that is temporary, committed, and focused. And all three are children of the new age in which management and communications are fluid and readily available for problem solving.

Does your team know your playbook?

This one comes straight from football. From experience and from information about the competition, a coach creates a playbook that contains detailed plans for actions or plays that the entire team must know without question and execute without pause in order to win games and advance toward the playoffs.

What is different about you as a manager? If you manage with your team knowing the intended results of each action, and if the members of the team have not honed their skills at execution of their tasks, then you are the coach without a playbook. And if you have a plan but do not share it with your direct reports, then they are acting without motivation toward mutual goals, without metrics to measure their progress toward the goals, and without the leadership that makes great winners.

So what does your business playbook look like? How do you create and update it? Who gets to see it? Again, there is a great parallel in football coaching. The coach creates a playbook from experience and research. He drills the team again and again in execution of the plays from memory and without pause. He keeps metrics for each team member to see, including yards gained, passes completed, games won. He compares these metrics to past seasons, to competitors, to his own lifetime bests.

You as a business leader are the coach for your team, no matter what the size. Trained employees execute their tasks better than those who are not. You are responsible for the training and for the outcomes both for individuals and the team. You set the goals and develop the metrics by which your team is measured against those goals. You publish the metrics, and use them to focus and align your team to perform even better.

You develop, train, measure, and reinforce successes, all based upon your coach's playbook. Unless of course you have no playbook and are just a fan in the stands without a clue, cheering for a team you know and love but do not effectively lead. All because of the playbook you should have created, shared, and used as your team's guide to success.

The Virtual Manager: It's all about your performance.

It is hard to hide incompetence behind appearance or personality when you are a virtual manager. In a virtual environment, people measure you mostly by your actions, and remember only the most recent good work you've done for them and for the organization.

Today, many companies hire great managerial talent who commute from a remote home location. Often, such senior managers start with a four-days-here, one-day-from-home plan that slowly degrades to two then sometimes three days operating remotely. And some senior managers are quite successful at driving innovation, vision and excellence from a distance. Some companies are operated entirely virtually and there is no other way to manage.

I'd suggest that the quality of a senior manager who must control from a distance must be higher than one always on the spot in front of middle management and staff. And I'd think that not every such remote manager is able to rise to the occasion, constantly creating a sense of urgency and a push for excellence in his or her absence. One thing is for sure. The risk of failure is higher when a manager is often absent from the scene of the problem, no matter how strong the person's skills at delegation and no matter how competent your employees are, one level down the ladder.

If you find yourself having to share your time between a distant location and home base, whether because of constant travel or living in a remote spot, you should redouble your energy - focusing your people at all levels toward being able to make decisions with skill and confidence. You should hone your skills of delegation with accountability, and practice your communication skills so that short communications count more than ever.

And you should find ways to focus your people upon your vision of excellence without seeming to merely be a cheerleader encouraging from the sidelines. Some great managers do this by keeping a mental or physical list of several, perhaps three, key performance indicators for each direct report, and quizzing about progress in regular planned or chance meetings. Others keep a dashboard that alerts them to excursions from expectation and permits more management by exception.

It's all about your performance, especially when you're physically absent some or much of the time. Take a few minutes to think about ways in which you can creatively leave yourself behind when you are absent, encouraging others to feel your sense of urgency directed toward achievement of your vision, even in your absence.

Virtual startups are no stigma.

Rent your first office with caution.

Recently, I became involved with a Southeast Asian company looking to expand into the United States. During the discussions with the CEO about hiring North American managers, he made it clear that he wanted us to find a first class office facility from which to start the search process, and proceeded to name cities that attracted him. Even after discouraging him from this backwards method of infrastructure-building, he kept bringing up the subject in subsequent months as new senior managers and sales people were hired, each starting with an orientation week at the Asian headquarters then returning to work from home. With audio and video conferencing and all the tools for communication and collaboration available today, each of these four new employees felt empowered, connected and enthused to work from home for the first time. The Asian CEO was still talking about finding an office when the natural progression of growth made it obvious that two of the four needed to be replaced. These two worked from homes in widely scattered cities. Had the office been located to accommodate either one, the company would have had to find replacements in the same geographical area as the office. Without that restriction, outstanding replacements were located based upon skill and experience, not location.

Very early stage businesses, start-ups, actually benefit from the establishment of a virtual environment. The flexibility in hiring decisions, reduced fixed costs, forced highly specific communications and better definition of job responsibilities that most often result from need, almost always give a virtual startup the edge financially and flexibly.

So can a startup exist for a reasonably long time as a virtual company? A decade ago there was a stigma that prevented many CEO's from thinking it possible. Today, virtual offices are accepted at all levels of many organizations of all sizes.

Well-managed employees work well from home.

Do home-based employees work with the same dedication and productivity as those in office cubicles next to each other? That depends upon the management as much as the employee. I have a friend who is a CEO of a recruiting firm who "virtualized" her company after a decade of maintaining a fixed office location. She organizes morning conference calls, has each employee tweet the others in their department when starting work and ending the day, creates the feel of closeness with employee contests, and rewards her best sales people by assigning them the best leads, creating an environment where the best excel and those unable to cut it in a virtual environment fall out on their own accord for lack of revenue. But most important, the unpredicted benefit of having very low infrastructure overhead may be the one most important element in saving the company during the strongest and longest downturn in recruiting industry memory because of the recent recession. Much larger recruiting companies are in trouble, with high fixed costs for facilities that cannot be shed quickly. This CEO's decision to try to retain an excellent, motivated staff in a virtual environment is paying off in every way. The employees are more satisfied, actually work more hours in a day even if spread over a longer period, and uniformly claim a better lifestyle as a result of the move.

But as you see from the story above, it does take more creative management to make this work. It is a management skill that was not taught nor learned until recent times. A creative CEO will find ways to motivate and compensate for the lone nature of working alone, but using social networking tools to make office workers and home workers feel and behave as a unit.   After all, with this generation of texting, tweeting, IM-based workforce, you'll find as much of this kind of communication from adjacent cubicles as from distant home offices.

Let's pause for a word about dress code and formal accountability for the home office worker. Employees working at home must dress for work, even if casual, and find a schedule for the start of each work day that is to be counted upon by fellow workers. It won't be long before home workers will routinely greet each other via video conference from the home desk. Although possible today and used by some, it is not a requirement of most employers with home-based workers. Someone who "comes to work each day" even if to the computer in a separate part of an apartment, is putting on the business hat in a much more formal way that one who drifts to a computer in the room beside a blaring TV, dressed in pajamas and arriving whenever convenient.

How about the employee unable to self-motivate in a home environment? With the proper measurements of productivity, it will soon become quite obvious to both the employee and manager that such an opportunity is not right for that person.

Ask any CEO who has tried letting employees work from home, whether for a day a week or as a rule with occasional office visits. You'll find stories of emails time stamped well into the night, work performed at unusual hours and productivity increases. You'll also hear a bit of pride in the telling. A CEO that encourages this once-risky venture and is rewarded with increased performance, is a person fulfilled and willing to tell anyone who'll listen.

Lead by consensus wherever possible.

Dictators are not great leaders in the long run. People follow such leaders by fear, rarely by devotion. Employees want to have a stake in their own destiny, and above all want to understand why actions are taken which affect them, even if the outcome is not in the employee's favor.

The best leaders are those who share problems and alternative solutions with their direct reports, then seek consensus in decisions as a result. Obviously, there are exceptions. If the group cannot agree upon a course of action, the leader must act, even if the action taken is to defer the decision until more information or a consensus is reached. And obviously, an emergency is rarely the time to seek consensus before acting to protect lives and assets.

In non-profit enterprises, such as educational institutions, the pace of decision-making is usually much slower as the executive director, president or chairman seeks consensus from the community wherever possible. Many business executives first joining a non-profit board are surprised by the slow speed of deliberation and the resulting consensus-seeking that results. Especially in collegiate academic communities, a dictator chancellor or president rarely lasts long in the position.

And this rule becomes a part of the DNA or culture of the organization. Employees throughout the organization want to feel empowered to make suggestions, to know the reasons for decisions that affect their jobs, to have some small control over their environment.

Without a doubt, if you interview employees and managers in companies large and small, you will find that those feeling most appreciated, most productive, and most creative are the ones allowed and encouraged to participate in the decisions that affect their jobs.

Turn "process" into "game."

Most of us are driven by the competitive spirit, the desire or need to win. It reinforces self-worth, provides closure at the end of a good effort, and energizes us during the effort to achieve.

Many of us as managers - and our employees as workers - are driven by process, actions required to achieve a result. And many of these actions are repetitive to a fault, contributing to boredom and ultimately to restlessness and desire for something new, in or out of the company.

There is a solution. Everyone loves a good game. It provides a short competitive experience with a measurable outcome in which the players know who won and by how much. And it challenges each player to play again with learned skills and an incentive to beat the past score.

So think of ways to make each process into a game, one in which there is a defined metric or measure of the winner at the end of a cycle short enough to permit teaching, celebration, challenge, and motivation for the next time played. Create small but meaningful competitions between groups or individuals for which recognition or small rewards are published in advance. Allow for wins to be accomplishments of the team, as much as the individual, so that competition is a team sport, not an individual play for power. Create and publish metrics as goals and comparisons to past accomplishments. And pause to celebrate each new first or top score.

There are so many places where routine jobs can be made into a game. Sales people know the rules and play to win, celebrating each small success along the way. Why not empower each person or manager of each task in other areas to create similar challenges and metrics? These cannot be viewed as corny or artificial ways for management to gain more output from a group without significant recognition or reward. Or you will risk a backlash in which employees see the effort as merely a way to increase productivity in disguise, with no reward worth the effort.

Be a good coach, and be creative. We all want to play to win and be recognized for our efforts.

Oh please! Walk the talk!

Ever had a manager who hung those motivational posters around the office, spoke of "pushing together," or "you're empowered to give great service" – and then acted at least once in complete disregard of those statements?

It takes only one time caught by subordinates to lose the faith of an entire group of faithful followers. And that certainly counts for customers too, although the customer jungle drums don't communicate quite as fast as the virtual water cooler system, even with today's many ways of posting negative reviews about company behavior.

On the other hand, there are great examples of managers who put their reputation or large amounts of company resources on the line to reinforce just such statements. Think of a surprising positive interaction you had with a call center employee or store clerk who resolved your problem and calmed your anger by exceeding your expectations. That happened to me recently when I made an off-handed complaint to a call center employee solving another problem for me and she immediately said, "I'll take care of that by crediting you in full for the cost of that unit." I was floored, and told dozens of people about the unexpected service offered without an angered demand or even a request for compensation.

How do you empower your people to actually do what you claim as your motto or standard of service? Some hotel chains have a policy that any desk clerk can make a problem right up to a cost of over a thousand dollars. Now that's showing faith.

I have told the story of a customer of our company whose facility was destroyed in a catastrophic fire which took with it all of the records of guests staying at and reserved to be coming to the property. The catch: the property was on a remote island in Australia, and the manufacturing plant in Southern California. Without a second thought, our people gathered to help the distraught property management recover data from backups, interview present guests, and quickly install the brand new computer diverted from another installation shipped overnight to theirs. The benefit to the customer was obvious as was their continuous praise for the company and our people in helping them in their hour of need. But just as important, the employees of the company participated as a unit in following the stated promise in our motto, "Customer first, always!"

Actions always speak louder than words. Always.

Setting your moral compass.

Almost all of us in our leadership roles are looked upon to provide clues for behavior by those who look up to us, whether family members or subordinates in the workplace or even those we associate with as peers, suppliers, or customers.

In your business and personal life, there will be moments that will define you forever in the eyes of those you might not be aware are watching. And nowhere is this more evident in the way you respond to issues where your actions require extraordinary sacrifice financially or in personal ambition.

If a clerk in a store gives you too much change from a sale where you paid cash, do you think before returning the overage? Is your decision effected by whether someone is with you and watching? If an error is made that results in a customer or office superior asking "who could have done this?," do you step up to take responsibility quickly to avoid casting the focus upon another person? If your company could achieve inordinate short term profit from the lack of knowledge on the other side in a new sale, do you take advantage of the moment and profit from the ignorance of the individual on the other side?

The temptation to do these things is great. But in every case the lasting negative effect is worse than the gain temporarily made. For the short term profit in reputation or financial gain, you have established one piece of evidence that you are not living by the golden rule, whether someone is watching or not. And somehow, there is always someone who finds out what you did, even if months later.

On the other hand, think of those individuals you trust to always make the right decision morally and ethically even when at great personal expense. Your respect for that person is unwavering, and you would defend and trust that person if called upon to do so, likely without question.

Your subordinates, employees, family members, and peers are looking to you to measure your moral compass and perhaps to point their way as well as yours. "Good people finish first" is a statement that requires a leap of faith that in the end, those that take advantage of others almost always find themselves behind those who step forward to do the right thing.

Start or maintain your business life with an unwavering moral compass. Doing so is not the quickest way to profit, but the most honorable and ultimately most rewarding in so many ways.

Build consensus.

Surely you've been exposed to articles, courses and lectures about various styles of management, and how each is appropriate for some companies and for some levels of organization and at some times. For example, a consensus-building leader works well in that style until someone yells "fire!," and the emergency requires a dictatorial style of management to act quickly, protecting lives.

If you've ever been on the board of a non-profit organization, especially one in education, you know that a dictatorial style of management has no place in the organization (again unless there is an emergency requiring life-saving decisions). In the non-profit sector, all decisions move slower, frustrating many board members who are business tycoons or entrepreneurs used to making rapid, final decisive moves in the workplace.

But wait a minute. Is it appropriate for managers in any business to make a habit of making rapid, decisive moves as a matter of style? In a past insight, I used the phrase: "Bet the farm only when the crops are on fire!" to underline the risk in making continuous bold decisions that obligate a company's resources in a single transaction.

It is much more appropriate and certainly more appreciated if you take the time to bring your direct reports along in the thinking process, to obtain their input with issues that affect them, and to attempt to gain consensus from the leadership team before moving into implementing decisions where risk is involved or where the others are affected. Many a time I have thought a solution was obvious until one of my board members, peers or direct reports pointed out a facet of the problem not previously considered. Bold decisions seem to reflect strong leadership. More often, they reflect a deficiency in willingness to cede power to the group unless for some reason necessary to withhold that power.

A decision made by consensus is probably a wiser decision and surely one that will be received down the line with more willingness to implement it than one posted as an order. Orders come from somewhere up there in the minds of most people below direct reports. And there is no better way to destroy a company's culture than having the majority of those in the workforce believing that they are just "workin' for the man" (woman) when they walk in the door.

Good management means great empowerment.

So, we've discussed why it is important to build consensus in an organization in most every major decision. To do so, a CEO must be able to relinquish some degree of power, overriding decisions made by consensus only with some thought and certainly with an explanation to those involved.

A manager secure in the position should never fear empowering direct reports to make decisions that fall within the resources allocated to them and within the budget agreed to with them. A micro-manager cannot cede that kind of authority, even within pre-arranged limits, and as a result meddles with decisions made by direct reports, removing authority from each whenever such moves are made, and rendering the individual more impotent in the eyes of that person's reports.

On the other hand, a great CEO or manager not only empowers his or her direct reports, s/he directs those people to do the same with their reports down the line. All this is done within limits that should seem obvious: financial impact has been provided for within the plan; and no other individuals or departments are affected negatively by such an empowered action without notice and involvement.

The more power you cede, the more you become a teacher and the more your direct reports grow in their positions. Further, the more you share your decisions, the more you prepare those below to assume your position if ever necessary or appropriate.

If you cannot or will not empower your direct reports, you must ask yourself: why? If it is insecurity that is the root cause, then the best course of action is to share the power even more quickly, as you'll look and feel more like the group is supportive of you and your position. If you are a micro-manager and are unwilling to allow those below to fail, even with more minor decisions, then you are restricting their growth in their positions, certainly causing dissatisfaction in their ranks, and missing the most important opportunities to enable scaling your organization to a much larger size.

Act like an Eagle Scout.

You may have been a Girl Scout or a Boy Scout in your youth. Certainly you are aware of the top rank in each – the Gold Award for girls and the Eagle badge for boys. Scouting teaches leadership and even if we were not members in our youth, there are lessons for us all.

For example, the Boy Scouts of America motto is "Be prepared." And from that comes training in first aid, disaster preparation, and outdoor skills, planning for events and outings, and any number of simulations or practice runs at rescue training – from snake bites to earthquakes to fires to broken limbs to heart attacks in the wilderness. We could learn from this simple oath taken by boys from ten to eighteen. Simply learning to ask "What if?" of our direct reports is a good first step toward reducing exposure to bad outcomes, whether attempting to plan for handling a natural disaster or workplace calamity.

Every Scout memorizes the twelve points of the Scout Law: A Scout is *trustworthy, loyal, helpful, friendly, courteous, kind, obedient, cheerful, thrifty, brave, clean, and reverent*. That may seem an overwhelming list of aspirations, but would it not be a better world if each of us practiced most, if not all, of these?

By the time a boy reaches Eagle Scout, he has internalized the Scout Oath and Scout Law to a degree many employers later recognize makes him a better candidate for a job merely by that attainment in his youth. After all, only two percent of all Boy Scouts do reach Eagle rank.

We adults cannot revisit our youth to live seven years of our lives with these principles always in close sight. But we can aspire to act like an Eagle Scout, an adult who recognizes the values and attempts to practice them in business and personal life for the betterment of ourselves and our companies.

Quality, Quantity, and Values – Rating Your Associates.

How often do you take the time to rate your employee-associates? Is it really worth the time and effort when measured from the perspective of the company and of the employee?

First, like any important process, the metrics used to measure effectiveness and progress are so important to a successful outcome, that a good manager will spend time reviewing those metrics used by others and create an appropriate set of measurements for your company that reflect the most important attributes of the employee as they relate to the needs of the company. There are many formats for use in rating and reviewing employees, and selection of the proper form and format is the first step in a successful process.

I've been asked often if such reviews should be performed quarterly, semi-annually, or annually. Note that few ever ask if they should be performed at all. When an employee is subsequently dismissed for any reason, the documentation of past performance and reviews, including any past notification of weaknesses or warnings, becomes an important shield to protect the company against a subsequent lawsuit or challenge from a state employee review process. Many companies do not take the time to perform such reviews, and end up paying the price in adverse rulings by courts or commissioners based upon verbal statements alone. So protection of the corporation is reason number one for investing in such a process.

Second, employees most often genuinely want to know how they are performing against the company's standard and management expectations. It is human nature to desire praise; and the review process is one tool to provide such positive feedback to employees.

Third, every employee should be directed to work toward the goals of his or her department, which in turn are aligned with those of the company itself. By providing a format for review that includes a number of key performance indicators that measure just such alignment, both the employee and the manager keep focused upon the real goals for productivity.

Fourth, corporate values are passed on to employees in a number of self-reinforcing ways, including discussion of values during the review process. Many a business would not have strayed into a dangerous regulatory and legal abyss if employees were shown, told, and measured by their adherence to the values stated by their corporation as important to all stakeholders.

To answer the question of how often to perform such employee reviews, from experience I suggest that quarterly formal written reviews are too much of a task for all. Semi-annual reviews are excellent, especially for companies that offer stock options as well as merit increases for outstanding performance. With such reviews, option grants could be tied to one review and merit increases to the other. Two carrots in a year are better than one for obtaining desired outcomes. The very minimum level of acceptability should be one annual review for an employee.

Review the CEO? I participate in a number of CEO reviews as board chair of those companies. In such reviews of the top executive, I reach out to his or her direct reports for input, and then I turn to other members of the board of directors. With such a comprehensive view of CEO performance, it is much easier to sit with the CEO and provide valuable input that is useful for CEO development. And even founder-CEO's are thankful for the input received, usually taking criticism as a challenge to grow in the position.

I'd have a difficult time thinking that any company, large or small, could perform at its peak without great employee metrics including individual key performance indicators, capped by consistent reviews and feedback.

Recalling the Lateral Arabesque: Retaining Valuable employees.

Funny how good messages come back in new forms after years of languishing out in the ether. Dr. Laurence J. Peter in *The Peter Principle: Why Things Always Go Wrong* wrote in the early 1960's of the "lateral arabesque," describing how companies promote incompetent employees sometimes by sending them to another department or division to get them out of the way of progress.

I use the term differently in a more poignant way to describe how companies rarely realize the true value of an employee until s/he jumps (the arabesque) to another company in a higher position, valued there financially and for skills which were taken for granted in the original company.

The twist ("double arabesque") is that the original company management only then realizes what the person is worth, and makes advances to bring him or her back at an even higher salary and more inflated title.

The moral is that great employees are never as valuable as when they leave and land at a better position elsewhere.

I've lived this experience time and again, most recently with the chief architect of a product line who jumped to a competitor for more money and more recognition. Remember that the grass IS almost always greener... The original company was afraid to upset the structure of its salary compensation schema and could not (would not) take the chance to raise the person's pay to be more than competitive early enough to show the love and trust deserved by the valuable player.

That's the quandary. Mature companies have structure and ranges of salaries that are baked in so carefully as to not disturb the ecosystem. How do you over-compensate the most valuable players? Additional stock options? Bonuses? Higher base pay? An increase in title? More attention? Each of these is a good tool and should be considered before needed to reward and encourage the best players before they can imagine playing for another team.

The irony of it all is that the lost person's replacement probably will be offered a starting salary higher – sometimes much higher – than the one paid to the departed player. And – to regain the one departed, an even higher offer will have to be made. Two jumps: a double arabesque. One initiated not just by the player, but by the largess of management.

Have you star players in danger of performing the dreaded lateral arabesque?

Avoid the recruiting boomerang.

It has happened to all of us who have been leaders in business long enough. One of your employees is approached by an employee of a customer or of a supplier, stating that "It sure would be great to work in your company." And without a policy or sometimes without thinking, your employee responds with a "Let me help," or worse yet, "I have a position open."

You should be clear from the start that no one at your company may offer a job to any current employee of a stakeholder - a customer, a partner in development or in distribution, or of a supplier. The rule should be one that includes only one "out": if a person resigns from the position with the stake-holding company, then you will be happy to talk about a position. No winking, sending signals, or quiet promises.

There are instances where such an existing stakeholder employee offers to go to his or her boss and ask permission to speak with you, and the boss not only concurs but agrees to call you (not just to take your call). In that case alone, it is proper to continue as far as the offer and beyond.

Let me tell you the story from one of my companies that recently learned about the recruiting boomerang the hard way. The CEO checked into a hotel that was a customer for its enterprise management system, and through a few innocent questions found that the owner was about to purchase several new systems for his new projects. The front desk clerk cheerfully gave the CEO the owner's contact information.

So the CEO called the owner that day. "I will never deal with your company again!" was the short reply from the owner to the CEO. It turns out that a manager from the CEO's company had recently thrown the recruiting boomerang at that very same cheerful clerk, hinting that a job would be available if she'd like to apply. The clerk told the owner, and the rest is history.

Properly, the CEO begged the owner for forgiveness, immediately sent an email to all managers reinforcing the existing policy of not hiring a stakeholder, and spoke to the person making the offer in a non-threatening tone, again reinforcing the policy. During the phone conversation with the owner, the CEO carefully set the stage for a later call to mend fences and check on progress with the existing system already installed. He made all the right moves given the situation.

But wouldn't it have been easier to avoid throwing the recruiting boomerang in the first place?

It is dangerous, but fair game to hire from a competitor.

Sometimes it is the first thought you or your managers have when in need of skilled talent, especially for sales or product development.

It is not hard to find and observe the best employees of a good competitor at work, skillfully moving the competitor forward in a visible way.

And it is a tempting slice of pie – two slices for one price – to take a critically needed employee from a competitor, damaging that firm while building yours.

The problem is that a visible hire that "cuts" the competitor makes the competitor's management bleed. And you've heard of blood revenge. That's the worst kind, because it results in emotionally lashing out at the offender (you) with a response that is greater than the action that precipitated it. In many cases, your firm can withstand the response. In some though, cross-raiding of employees by offering unsustainable salaries or perks you cannot offer to all because of your size and financial position will leave you in a position to pay grandly for your action.

Consider the relative size of the competitor, the visibility of the target employee, and your ability to withstand a backlash before exercising the two slice tactic.

Develop a culture of curiosity.

Some of the world's best companies to work for are those that encourage employees to spend time following their own paths of curiosity toward development of new products or services. *Google, 3M, Facebook*, and *Microsoft* all allow their employees to take time to explore new ideas they conceive and attempt to develop.

Famously, the post-it note is an example of such a product coming from employees of 3M who were looking for quite another market for their newest light adhesive product. And many free products and services have been spawned by Google employees working during their one-day-a-week personal curiosity time.

It is an opportunity that is open to any CEO to encourage creative thinking, problem solving, product creation, efficiency-creation among the troops. Rewards don't have to be financial, but certainly, when the gains are measured in dollars, that seems appropriate when the new development is not just a part of the job specification for a creative employee with a great idea.

Every company has hidden talent, creative thinkers that are not in a position to demonstrate their talents. CEO's often focus employees on the company's goals, without allowing time to explore the edges to create alternative solutions, or to think ahead toward new possibilities.

What if you encouraged each of your associates to spend ten percent of their time working alone or with others on cost-saving or efficiency improvements, sketching new ideas for products or changes to products that they may not be directly involved in creating? What if that refreshing opportunity actually were to make each person return to the assigned job with a fresh new look and appreciation for the creative time spent? It could happen, but only if you as manager develop the culture of curiosity that makes such creativity a part of your company DNA.

Be a leader!

This simple statement is not what it seems at first. I quote this from a frequent family exhortation by parent to child in the Kemp clan, going back several generations. The late Jack Kemp, famous as quarterback for the Buffalo Bills and later as US Secretary of Housing and Urban Development then Vice Presidential candidate, told this story about his mom, as he continued the tradition with Jack's now-grown family.

"Be a leader!" each would say as they sent their offspring out into the world each morning. As Jack explained it, the call was not for his children to lead in the traditional sense, but to enable others to grow and prosper – the definition of true servant leadership.

This short statement is a reminder of what it means to be a great leader – to focus upon the welfare and growth of one's peers and subordinates.

Think of what internalizing that and making it true would do in this business world. There would be no office politics, no suspicion of the intent or hidden agenda about management, no wasted time protecting that part of the anatomy we must protect when making many of our decisions in management.

Used in this context, servant leadership turns the leadership pyramid upside down, causing each level nearer the customer to have more empowerment to serve the customer than the level formerly above it.   Nordstrom, Zappos, and an increasing number of retail-centric companies practice this religiously.   It may not be appropriate for your enterprise at this time or in this niche, but it certainly is always appropriate in your family and social lives.

"Be a leader!"

Document your tribal knowledge.

It is not common for the CEO of a rapidly growing company to think of slowing down the furious pace enough to have each manager (including the CEO) document the job process managed, as well as see to the documentation for each process managed below.

And it is even more of a challenge to consider documenting the tribal knowledge of a company's key employees. Examples include forcing the entire sales and customer support team to use a single database such as SalesForce or Sugar or Act to document the interactions with prospects and customers, or using "REM" statements liberally inside software code to notify future coders of critical information contained and reasons for making code branches, assigning variables with unusual names or more.

As CEO, have you made a list of your critical chain of advisors, including bankers, accountants, industry advisors, and more? Do you have a "secret spot" for critical information someone might need if you were incapacitated or worse? Especially when we are young, we feel invincible, and documenting tribal knowledge seems a chore with no reward.

Then inevitably a key employee gives notice and we begin to worry over what knowledge we will watch walk out that door, wonder how we will recover in the short term and grow out of the problem in the long term. We worry that asking our subordinates to document their processes will look like the first step in removing them from their job. And we worry over lost productivity during this effort.

But if we make this a part of the culture of the corporation starting at the top and from an early point in the life of the organization, this process becomes an accepted way in which managers learn and leave behind, able to move up the chain with minor disruption both in the job left behind and the job assumed. It makes for a smoother process for seeking outside hires by providing a model for the job specification to be written.

And it allows everyone to better appreciate the organization, understanding the limits of each position and the duties performed, avoiding conflicts between managers when in the future changes are made in the organization and in personnel during periods of growth or even downsizing.

Tribal knowledge is an asset of the corporation, to be protected as much as cash in the bank.

Avoid the office politics trap.

It is hard to separate this kind of advice from economic lessons in running a business, when office politics can threaten a business in ways that are subtle, but sometimes just as devastating as economic shocks or continuing poor management.

Most any office with more than one level of management (more than ten employees) can become a Petri dish for office politics. It may be human nature to attempt to gain the good graces of one's superior in the work place. But it is a perverse form of human nature to do so at the expense of others. Some employees disrupt a business intentionally in order to gain attention and an advantage over fellow employees.

Other times, people with personal agendas or personal dislikes of other individuals will disrupt the harmony of an office environment with negative statements, rumors, and damning comments. We've all seen this unhealthy form of human activity in an office environment at one time or another.

So here's the advice: Never repeat, encourage, or even listen to the personal attacks by one individual against another within the organization. The first time you join in the conversation instead of stopping it, the first time you nod in agreement, the first time you take a side as a manager –is the last time you rule over an office-politics-free organization.

A boss has power that person doesn't often realize s/he has, when viewed from the lens of a subordinate. That power becomes perverse when a boss takes a side in any disagreement that is personal as opposed to business-problem oriented. The result is almost always hurt, frustration and anger from the party on the wrong end of such manager reinforcement, and a loss of work time and certainly good will toward the organization and toward management itself.

To set the example by stopping the personal attack, refocusing the parties on productive work and moving on is to state by your words and actions that you will not tolerate such behavior in the work place. To ignore such action when observed is to allow one person or a small group to undermine the organization in subtle steps that can only increase in size and effect.

Worse yet, to take a side in a personal dispute is to reduce your authority and alienate one person or group and reinforce bad behavior.

Hone your sense of urgency!

It is an unfortunate truism that most of us become a bit stale in our jobs after some time, even if we are most successful at it and appreciated by all who work for or with us. It is human nature to start in a new position with enthusiasm, lofty goals, new ideas, and a heightened awareness of those around us and their ideas for the business.

And it is equally human for anyone to become complacent to some degree after an initial flurry of effort, ideas, reorganizations, brilliant decisions, and early successes. Complacency is relative. There is no direct measure to determine when a manager, even the CEO, has run out of new ideas and that sense of heightened awareness. Usually this is masked by our having a better grip on the real drivers of the business, able to quickly see when things are not going right or people not performing to their peak.

But think back to those first days on the job. You were ready and willing to effect change, to listen to anyone, to take in ideas, and share yours with your peers. You spent extra hours more often in creative efforts, encouraged discourse, and delved into new ideas and projects with enthusiasm.

You exhibited a sense of urgency that charged your direct reports, made you want to come to work every day refreshed, and demonstrated to all that something special was happening in their world.

Can you honestly state that your sense of urgency remains today at the same level as when you first started at this position? Few of us could, and that is the reason why investors often feel that turnover in executive ranks is not so bad after all. The average life of a CEO in the position is shorter today than ever before, partly because investors expect continual acceleration, and partly because a person seems to have only so much new material to offer. If each of us could maintain that same sense of urgency that drove us to succeed early on, our peers, direct reports, investors, and stakeholders would all notice and respond accordingly.

Challenging your peers and reports to come up with new ideas, solutions, projects, and improvement in processes – all are signs of a good manager still in control of his or her sense of urgency. It is hard for those around you to slack off with such a whirlwind adjacent.

I have previously told the story of the successful CEO who drove to work each Monday morning asking himself, "What if this were my first day on the job as CEO? What would I do?" He kept his company and his peers always thinking ahead, if nothing else to prevent his surprising them with ideas and solutions to problems that should have been uncovered and acted upon earlier.

It is not an easy task - reinventing yourself to be that person you were on the first day, but with the knowledge and experience since gained. But it is an important part of being a great manager and retaining the focus upon excellence that certainly drove you to succeed back then.

Move your team from competence to excellence.

When a new CEO or manager is hired into a company, for a while lots of energy flows from the top and new ideas seem to be generated daily. It is one reason not to fear the unknown when upper level management long in place turns over, often leaving most everyone worrying over how they'll ever do without their lost leader.

The problem seems to come after everyone settles back into some sort of normalcy and the new senior manager becomes comfortable in his or her position. There is a natural momentum in most companies, one that is usually slow and deliberate. New ideas are vetted carefully, run by a number of departments, considered from many angles and implemented with deliberation. The temporary enthusiasm for cutting through the old way of doing things calms employees into an acceptance that little has changed over time.

The real opportunity for a leader to raise the bar is in the consistency of his or her vision and willingness to accept change for the benefit of the organization. This is true especially when the company is making its numbers and problems are few. There is nothing wrong with consistency. It brings a normalcy to everyone's jobs that most people welcome.   But that normalcy often comes inside a creative vacuum. Competitors often jump into holes created by slowing innovation.

I've told the story about Bill Conlin before, but it is worth repeating. Bill was the CEO of CalComp, a Lockheed company. Most every Monday morning as he drove to work, he'd force himself to think: "What if this was my first day on the job, and I could make changes without worrying over the past?" Bill's managers feared those Mondays they say, because that hard-driving enthusiasm for change, for excellence, was like a lightning bolt upsetting the old way on occasion and bringing fresh ideas to the front for consideration and execution.

How many of us fall into the comfortable routines of management, thinking that we have this job down to a science, with the operation running smoothly and without need for much intervention? How many of us have fallen a few notches on the excellence scale over time, accepting our environment as of the last change, happy with ourselves for past achievements toward upping the enterprise?

What would you do if you were new at the job and had no restriction upon the changes you could make for the good of the company? Is there redundancy in levels of management that you've tolerated too long? Has the product or service not gained ground against its competitors of late? Are you sure of your marketing and pricing positioning? What about the training and competency of your operational staff?

Want to reinvigorate yourself in your job? Make next Monday morning's drive a creative thinking exercise in upping your game in your personal fight for excellence.

Finally, in a downturn, and there will be downturns that match the economy when a company begins to mature, recurring revenues can and often will save the company itself and smooth the revenues through the downturn.

If you have not spent considerable time refining a strategy to include recurring revenues, do so now. And remember, that once annual contracts are in place, they must include escalation clauses based upon some cost index to prevent their profitability from declining involuntarily over the years as inflation eats into the value of each non-indexed contract.

Time does fly when you're having fun. Lighten up for maximum lift.

Have you ever noticed how slow time passes when you are in a troubled environment? Conversely, sometimes you look up at the end of a great day and wonder where the time went. Over the years, I have discovered that the difference is not just applicable to the good times, but to the environment, created by the senior executives, that filters throughout the organization. Every time, a corporate work culture encouraging humor causes employees to enjoy their work, spend more time with associates, and laugh many more times through the day.

At one point in our mutual careers, my brother located his growing architectural practice just a mile from my record company in West Hollywood, California. I would visit his office and immediately notice an atmosphere of "joyous creativity" throughout the organization. Every cubicle was decorated with whimsical drawings, posters, kid's creativity, and more. As I walked through the facility, I could hear laughter emanating from cubicles, almost constant as a background song of simple joy at work. Those visits were wonderful times to recharge my batteries, and I was not even a part of the company. Imagine how they affected the attitude and creativity of those working there. Think of how clients loved to associate with their counterparts in such an environment.

Try as I could to reproduce such an environment, my company was too spread out, the background noises of manufacturing too loud to make the same environment possible. The best I could do was touch individuals and small groups with that same joy of the journey, adding humorous opportunities for lightening up as often as possible.

But after all these years, I will never forget the magic of that architectural office, and how much everyone there wanted not to let it ever slip away.

Take every opportunity to lighten up, to ease the often-self-imposed pressures of constant work, to unlock more of the creativity of your workforce through the use of appropriate humor. What a lift that brings.

About the author...

Dave Berkus has a proven track record in operations, venture investing and corporate board service, both public and private. As an entrepreneur, he has formed, managed and sold successful businesses in the entertainment and software arenas. As a private equity investor, he has obtained healthy returns from liquidity events in over a dozen investments in early-stage ventures. As a corporate mentor and director, he was named *"Director of the Year"* for his directorship efforts with over 40 companies in the past decade.

Dave was the founder of **Computerized Lodging Systems Inc.,** *(CLS),* which he guided as founder and CEO for over a decade that included two consecutive years on the *Inc.500* list of America's fastest growing companies, expansion to six foreign subsidiaries and twenty-nine foreign distributors, while capturing 16% of the world market for his enterprise products. Known as a hospitality industry visionary with many "firsts" to his credit and for his accomplishments in advancing technology in the hospitality industry, in 1998 he was inducted into the **Hospitality (HFTP)** **"International Hall of Fame,"** one of only thirty so honored worldwide over the years.

He has made over 80 investments in early stage ventures, for which he has an IRR of 97%, which includes capital contributions to his two funds (**Berkus Technology Ventures, LLC** and **Kodiak Ventures, L.P.**, for which he is the managing partner). He is also Chairman Emeritus of the Tech Coast Angels, one of the largest angel networks in the United States.

In recognition for adding significant shareholder value for emerging technology companies over the past decade, he was named **"Director of the Year-Early Stage Businesses"** by the *Forum for Corporate Directors* of Orange County, California and **"Technology Leader of the Year"** by the Los Angeles County Board of Supervisors. Dave currently sits on ten corporate boards and four non-profit boards.

Dave is also a senior partner in the twenty year old consulting firm of *Hospitality Automation Consultants, LTD (HACL)*, and lends his considerable visionary and strategic talents to worldwide hospitality chains and groups. He is the partner responsible for business process reorganization, strategic planning, software development and wide-area network infrastructure, and enterprise management systems.

A graduate of Occidental College, Dave currently serves as a Trustee of the College. Aside from this book, he is author of the first *"BERKONOMICS"* and its accompanying workbook, *"Extending the Runway"* published by Aspatore Press, and co-author of *"Better Than Money!"*- all books for emerging growth technology company executives. Dave serves as Board Member of the San Gabriel Valley Council of *Boy Scouts of America*, Board Member of the *Forum for Corporate Directors*, and is Chairman of the Advisory Board of the technology arm of the *ABL Organization*, a networking organization of CEOs in high tech businesses.

He is often engaged as keynote speaker for events worldwide, speaking on trends in technology and of legal and practical issues of governance for emerging company corporate boards.

To contact Mr. Berkus for speaking engagements or workshops, email dberkus@berkus.com , or phone (626)355-5375.

Dave's books are available for purchase from the above website, or the same source from which this book was purchased.

Subscribe to the free weekly email or blog, www.Berkonomics.com, containing much of the information from Dave's books with lots of comments from readers with their own stories to tell.

Follow Dave on Twitter (@daveberkus) and Facebook (Dave.Berkus).

Other books by Dave Berkus available directly from *www.berkus.com* or from your favorite bookseller or online store:

EXTENDING THE RUNWAY
Aspatore Press / Thompson West Publications

The five tools board members and executives can use to help their companies succeed.   How boards and CEOs should relate to each other for growing the enterprise. Fifty-eight critical questions boards and management should consider in order to assure their mutual alignment.

BERKONOMICS
Hard cover, soft cover and eBook editions

Volume one of this series. One hundred and one critical insights for entrepreneurs, CEOs and board members covering the life of the company from ignition through liquidity event.   Dave tells over fifty stories to illustrate his insights, culled from his experience as entrepreneur and service on over forty corporate and ten non-profit boards.

BERKONOMICS WORKBOOK
Companion to BERKONOMICS, this very personal journal contains 101 exercises for the CEO or manager that make each of the insights contained in BERKONOMICS come to life in the form of provocative and actionable questions to be answered right on the pages of the workbook. Once completed, this workbook becomes the manager's personal blueprint for business growth.

ADVANCED BERKONOMICS
Hard cover, soft cover and eBook editions

Volume two of this series. One hundred and one critical insights for entrepreneurs, CEOs and board members covering the life of the company from ignition through liquidity event.   More advanced insights into planning and measurement for success with small business startups.

SMALL BUSINESS SUCCESS SERIES
A Series of eight short and inexpensive books or eBooks

Take all the great material in the BERKONOMICS series and slice it by subject, and you'll have these eight inexpensive, short books about issues that you and your management team needs to focus upon today. Ideal for giving to your entire management group for group discussions and business planning sessions.

BOOKS and eBOOKS IN THIS SERIES:

1. *Starting Up!*
2. *Raising Money*
3. *Positioning for Success*
4. *Managing your Workforce*
5. *Protecting your Business*

6. *Growing your Business*
7. *Building Great Boards*
8. *Cashing Out!*

www.ingramcontent.com/pod-product-compliance
Lightning Source LLC
Chambersburg PA
CBHW030009190526
45157CB00014B/1620